Don't let life's events and circumstances take a toll on you...

Talk to us today!

FRAGRANCE *of* GRACE
INTERNATIONAL

FAITH-BASED COUNSELING CENTER

We provide faith-based counseling that helps teenagers, young adults, women, and men overcome life's challenges as they apply the principles of God's word, professional, and clinical advice to whatever issues they may be dealing with.

We have a team of compassionate, trained and licensed professionals whose skills and prayers are channeled to see you gain mastery and recovery in whatever you may be experiencing in your life.

We strongly believe that you can overcome whatever it is you are going through as we work together to make your recovery a reality.

VISION:
To make recoveries from life's circumstances a reality, through faith-based counseling and clinical referrals.

OUR GOAL:
Our one goal, is to make your recovery a reality!

...making your
recovery a reality!

COUNSELING OFFERED

- Life Management Skills (Leadership, Entrepreneurship, Career Advise, Personal Development etc)
- Pre-marital & Marital
- Relationship Management
- Divorce & Separation
- Anxiety and Depression
- Co-Dependence & Self Esteem
- Anger Management
- Addictions: Drugs, Alcohol, Sex, other Habits
- Mental Health
- Behavioral Issues
- Grief/Loss Recovery
- Family/Parenting issues
- Starting All Over
- Stress Management
- Suicidal Thoughts
- General Guidance

TESTIMONIALS:

> I've had several pre-marital counseling with Pastor Joel. The services provided were phenomenal, I would highly recommend him to anyone. ~ Kernesha

> Faith based counseling puts you right on track and counselling done the right way! Fragrance of grace delivered this to me when I needed it. Thanks so much. ~ Olufunmilayo

To speak with one of our faith-based counselors, or book an appointment, please call: **+1 (443) 949-9815, (240) 3348144** or send us an email to: **fbcounseling@fragranceofgrace.org** or **fgicounseling@gmail.com.**

Website
fragranceofgrace.org/pages/faith-based-counseling

P.S: *All counseling sessions are at no cost, but we accept gifts and donations to continue to provide these services to more people. Thank you for your generosity.*

FRAGRANCE OF GRACE INTERNATIONAL Faith-Based Counseling Center.
...making your recovery a reality!

Address: 34 Defense Street, Suite 100, Annapolis, MD 21401, United States.

Registered Member of

EVERYDAY FRAGRANCE

365 Days of Daily Meditations and Devotional

Everyday is a gift!

May you gain the strength to overcome life's
hurts, habits, and hurdles everyday!

Joel Osebor

All scripture quotations in this book are from the Bible.

Scripture quotations from Aramaic Bible, Berean Standard Bible, Christian Standard Bible, Amplified Bible, Amplified Bible Classic Edition, Contemporary English Version, Easy-to-Read Version, English Standard Version, Geneva Bible, Good News Translation, God's Word, Holman Christian Standard Bible, KJV, International Children's Bible Version, International Standard Version, Jubilee Bible (2000), Living Bible, New American Standard Bible, New Century Version, New Heart English Bible, New Life Version, New. International Version, NET Bible, Philips Bible, The Message, The Passion Translation, Wycliffe Bible Translators, Weymouth New Testament, Young's Literal Translation.

Table of Contents

About EVERYDAY FRAGRANCE

These 365 days of daily meditations and devotional will be your road map to an endless path of possibilities. It contains topics such as the existence of God, relationships, mental health issues like grief & loss, crisis & trauma, fear, anxiety, depression, codependency, a crisis of faith, faith, personal development, planning, goal setting, having a positive mental attitude, time management, healthy self-esteem, speaking the right words, developing a goodly nature, making choices, discovering purpose, maximizing your potentials, and so many other issues that we engage with every day.

These inspired writings were from a place of struggles, hurts, hope, healing, and recovery. I believe they will make each day count for you as you experience sweet fragrance in every situation of life.

Part of the profit from sales of this book will be committed to supporting Mental Health Coaching programs, Prison programs, Food & Clothes Banks, School Projects, Homeless/Shelter Programs, and Youth Development Initiatives.

Author's Prologue

I wrote these daily meditations and personal devotional guide during a time in my life when I was going through my healing process from the loss of a loved one, coming to terms with the reality of starting all over again - marriage, career, purpose and so many other events that were happening in my world. These were traumatic situations in my life. I was going through a mental health and faith crisis and did not know what to do.

Everyday Fragrance captures my journey of hope, healing, recovery, and growth, which I believe are key needs in our world today. Over 90% of the world population will suffer one form of trauma in their lifetime. Few paths can truly bring wholeness to you. I found mine from connection to great people, friends, serving, and obedience to God.

I hope and pray that these thoughts inspired and captured by my experiences in this simple and easy-to-read book, will bring hope, healing, recovery, and growth to you too.

I look forward to reading your e-mail on how you're overcoming your life struggles and how we can share our experiences with our hurting world in need of hope, healing, and recovery.

This book is dedicated to your healing, recovery, and growth in and through all of life's circumstances!

Joel Osebor

+1(443) 949-9815

joel.osebor@fragranceofgrace.org

January 1: The Beginning

Life comes with its challenges and opportunities, allowing us to press for what we desire in every circumstance. It does not matter how it may seem; every situation presents a new beginning, as each new day, week, month, and year opens vast possibilities.

1. "In the beginning, God (Elohim) created [by forming from nothing] ..." (Genesis 1:1a Amplified)

New beginnings hand over a clean slate to you. And you have been given the inner will and raw materials – "words & thoughts" to print on the slate. The beginning with God is still in existence because He used His words.

You have a new beginning; USE YOUR WORDS to create your world in this new year!

MEDITATION FOR THE DAY: MY FATHER AND GOD, THANK YOU FOR A NEW YEAR; IT IS THE BEST YEAR EVER, IN JESUS' NAME!

January 2: You are not Alone

The beginning of a journey comes with a lot of uncertainty and fear of the unknown. Every beginning is formless and empty, all you can see or hold on to is the possibilities of the end in mind through hope, faith, visions, and dreams.

1. "The earth was formless and void or a waste and emptiness, and darkness was upon the face of the deep [primeval ocean that covered the unformed earth] ..." (Genesis 1:2a Amplified)

The journey of life at every new phase comes with its challenges that unsettles and keeps you awake at night. The weight of what you need to do, and the process can make the task ahead daunting.

Do not fret yourself out, there is one who promised to always be with you in and through all of life's journey. You are not alone!

MEDITATION FOR THE DAY:

THANK YOU, FATHER, FOR BEING WITH ME, IN THIS NEW YEAR, IN JESUS' NAME!

January 3: He is in You

As we begin each journey of different paths in life – family, relationships, career, business, ministry, or any life path, we can rarely tell what the outcomes will be. The only assurances we have are the instincts or nudging we feel in our hearts on the next step.

1. "… and the Spirit of God was moving over the surface of the waters." (Genesis 1:2b NASB)

Our paths in life are made easy when our relationship with the Spirit of God is strengthened daily. For every journey or path, we seek to pursue, God has already gotten to the end.

Yield your endeavors to the Holy Spirit, He knows the paths, and above all - He lives in You!

MEDITATION FOR THE DAY:

HOLY SPIRIT, I YIELD MY LIFE'S PATHS INTO YOUR HANDS, IN JESUS' NAME!

January 4: God Spoke Light

Life's journeys can be filled with dark paths that come in the form of doubts, fears, uncertainties, confusion, and cluelessness. As darkness cannot withstand light, these seemingly dark paths cannot resist the power of your words.

1. "God spoke: "Light!" And light appeared" (Genesis 1:3 The Message)

Life and situations are framed by words. God transforms our lives through His written and spoken words (do not underestimate the power of the BIBLE). Your journey in life will be framed by the words you speak – whether negative or positive.

When you Speak what God speaks, you will get the results God gets!

MEDITATION FOR THE DAY:

HOLY SPIRIT, LIGHT MY PATHS THIS NEW YEAR, WITH YOUR WORDS OF LIFE, IN JESUS' NAME!

January 5: Speak Good Things

The tribulations in our world today are real. Most things we see, hear, and experience leave us with negativity and impressions of bitterness, sorrow, and impossibilities. We just want to give up on life's possibilities. Do not dwell on the negatives, instead:

1. "… my friends, fill your minds with those things that are good and that deserve praise: things that are true, noble, right, pure, lovely, and honorable." (Philippians 4:8. Good News Translation)

The truth in life is this: "what you think about, you speak about, and you bring about". The things you speak about aid your journey in life. The BIBLE contains great things that speak excellent things concerning you.

Speak good things and expect great things!

MEDITATION FOR THE DAY:

HOLY SPIRIT, RENEW MY MIND, MY THOUGHTS, AND MY WORDS, IN JESUS' NAME!

January 6: Set Your Priorities

As we journey in life, there are valid, authentic, and attractive things that have the power to distract us. So many choices to select from, so many things to do, and so many realities to contend with. What you set as priorities determines your pace.

1. "But more than anything else, put God's work first and do what he wants. Then the other things will be yours as well." (Matthew 6:33 CEV)

I cannot emphasize enough the power in Matthew 6:33! Making God your top priority is your access to all that you will ever need in life. I am a humbled recipient of the truth of God's word.

Dear friend, make God your top priority, and every other thing will fall into place. I do not know how, but it works!

MEDITATION FOR THE DAY:

HOLY SPIRIT, GIVE ME THE GRACE TO DO GOD'S WORK FIRST, IN JESUS' NAME!

January 7: Doing God's work

Many of us wonder what it takes to do God's work. Some of us think going to church, giving our tithes, and acknowledging the deity of God or Jesus is God's work. Certainly, these are part of it. Jesus gave some light on this:

1. "Then they asked him, "What must we do to perform God's works? Jesus answered them, this is God's work: to believe in the one whom he has sent." (John 6:28-29. International Standard Version)

To believe in the one God sent involves our total commitment and devotion to what He stands for. His genuine love and devotion to God, and to serving others, He expects from us.

You do the works of God by obeying His words, serving others, and fulfilling your purpose on earth.

MEDITATION FOR THE DAY:

HOLY SPIRIT, HELP ME TO BE DEVOTED TO GOD, AND SERVE OTHERS, AS I FULFIL MY PURPOSE ON EARTH.

January 8: Masterpiece

A masterpiece is a work of outstanding artistry, skill, or workmanship. Dear friend, as you journey through the tides of life, never forget that you are God's greatest piece done with extraordinary skill. "For we are God's masterpiece. He has created us anew in Christ Jesus, so we can do the good things he planned for us long ago." (Ephesians 2:10. New Living Translation)

Pray:

Thank you, Lord, for making me your masterpiece in all of creation!

Thank you, Holy Spirit, for being my guide, strength, and helper in life's journey in Jesus' name!

MEDITATION FOR THE DAY:

THANK YOU, FATHER, FOR THE GLORY AND VICTORIES OF THIS YEAR IN JESUS' NAME!

January 9: Word-Ruled World

The daily operations of our human lives and our world are run on the platform of communication. And our communication embodies the power of negative and positive words that propel our actions or inactions. Our world is ruled by words!

1. "… he upholds the universe by the word of his power". (Hebrews 1:3 ESV)

Whether in politics, religion, commerce, relationships, media, arts, sports, and entertainment, words drive our lives. The words we speak dominate the outcomes we get. With words, our dreams and aspirations are achieved; with words, our lives can be broken.

What kind of words rule your life?

MEDITATION FOR THE DAY:

HOLY SPIRIT, LET THE WORD OF GOD DWELL RICHLY IN ME, LET IT RULE MY WORLD IN JESUS' NAME!

January 10: Words Build

As the quality of building materials is vital for the construction of a solid inhabitable structure, so also our words are vital for the building of our lives, and that of others. Your words reveal your thoughts, your thoughts shape your life.

"Let my words and my thoughts be pleasing to you..." (Psalms 19:14 CEV)

Every word you speak carries weight. It goes through a quality assurance process in the invincible realm. Any word you speak that is not pleasing to God, fails the quality test. Let your words build – let them build the reality you want in your life, and the life of others.

Resist the urge to destroy yourself and others with words.

MEDITATION FOR THE DAY:

HOLY SPIRIT, LET MY WORDS BE PLEASING TO YOU, IN JESUS' NAME!

January 11: Words Bring Forth

The words we speak operate at two levels. The first level is in the realm of imagination, vision, or the supernatural. The second level is the level of realization when the words we have spoken come into our physical realm or reality.

"When he spoke, the world was created; at his command, everything appeared" (Psalms 33:9 Good News Translation)

Your words can bring to pass the things you speak. Remember this always, you are a spirit being, the only creature that has the capacity to function in two realms at the same time.

Whatever you speak about, you bring about – your words bring into your life the things you have spoken and will speak!

Watch your words!

MEDITATION FOR THE DAY:

HOLY SPIRIT, LET MY WORDS BRING FORTH POSITIVE RESULTS IN MY LIFE, IN JESUS' NAME!

January 12: Words Produce Fruits

Life is governed by both moral and spiritual laws or principles. These Laws and principles are boundaries that guarantee the outcomes of our actions or inactions. The use of your words is one of them. Your words are seeds that produce fruits.

1. "A person will be satisfied with good from the fruit of his words…" (Proverbs 12:14a NET Bible)

Your words are in sync with the law of sowing and reaping. Good words produce good fruits; bad words produce bad fruits.

Watch your words, your next harvest is tied to the seed words you have sown or will sow!

MEDITATION FOR THE DAY:

HOLY SPIRIT, LET MY SEED WORDS BE YOUR INSPIRED WORDS, IN JESUS' NAME!

January 13: Words Kill

Every word we speak is armed with the ability to cause harm or to bring hope to us and others. No words that you speak are idle of their effects. They are intended to cause a negative or positive response. You carry life and death in your mouth.

1. Words kill, words give life; they are either poison or fruit—you choose (Proverbs 18:21 The Message)

We live in a world where it is impossible not to experience hurt and disappointments from others. But we should never use our words to kill or destroy others, even ourselves. Let this be your prayer daily: "Help me to guard my words whenever I say something." (Psalms 141:3 Contemporary English Version).

MEDITATION FOR THE DAY:

HOLY SPIRIT, LET MY WORDS GIVE LIFE TO ME AND OTHERS, IN JESUS' NAME!

January 14: Words Give Life

There is life and death in the words that we speak. In other words, the words that we speak can bring hope or discouragement to ourselves and others. Words are spiritual, they are controlled and empowered by the realm of the invincible.

1. "Life is spiritual. Your physical existence does not contribute to that life. The words that I have spoken to you are spiritual. They are life." (John 6:63 God's Word Translation)

There is no better time in history that we all need words filled with the spirit and life of God. Many of us are under financial, emotional, physical, mental, and spiritual attacks.

Only words empowered with the life of God can set us free!

MEDITATION FOR THE DAY:

HOLY SPIRIT, LET MY WORDS BE FILLED WITH YOUR LIFE AND POWER, IN JESUS' NAME!

January 15: Words Liberate

Many people are struggling in their lives because of the damaging consequences of words spoken against them. Many of us are under the siege of bullying, racial prejudice, abuse from parents, unpleasant and abusive relationships, and curses. All these can be changed in a short while.

1. "Do not use harmful words, but only helpful words, the kind that builds up and provides what is needed, so that what you say will do good to those who hear you." (Ephesians 4:29 God News Translation)

You can change the course of your future, by speaking helpful words to rebuild your life and others.

The thoughts and words of God, written in the BIBLE, are your timeless word-reconstruction materials to liberate yourself and others!

MEDITATION FOR THE DAY:

HOLY SPIRIT, LET YOUR WORDS LIBERATE ME FROM MY PAST NEGATIVE EXPERIENCES, IN JESUS' NAME!

January 16: Word Pollution

Oh, how we take the words we say for granted! The rate at which we curse, speak unpleasant words, make derogatory remarks about others, and the way we speak so lowly or puffy about ourselves, pollutes us. And the state of your heart plays a major role in this.

1. "The food you put into your mouth doesn't make you unclean and unfit to worship God. The bad words that come out of your mouth are what make you unclean." (Matthew 5:11 CEV)

Words are like water. They can either be fresh for drinking or too smelly, and harmful to drink.

The state of our lives reflects the level of word pollution in it!

MEDITATION FOR THE DAY:

HOLY SPIRIT, PURIFY MY HEART, LET MY WORDS BE GRACIOUS, IN JESUS' NAME!

January 17: Words Shape Destiny

The experiences of more than half of the world's population can be traced to the influence of words. Whoever we are, whatever we have become, and what we will be, have a direct relationship with the impact of words. The words we speak matter.

1. "A person's words can be a source of wisdom, deep as the ocean, fresh as a flowing stream." (Proverbs 18:4 Good News Translation)

The words we hear provide the resources to chart our life course. The success of a marriage, business, career, and other areas of our lives are driven by words. What you say shapes your destiny. If you want to see changes in your life, change the contents of your words.

The BIBLE is your source for life-changing words!

MEDITATION FOR THE DAY:

HOLY SPIRIT, LET MY WORDS CARRY YOUR LIFE-CHANGING INFLUENCE, IN JESUS' NAME!

January 18: Be a Wordsmith

God wants you and me to be a wordsmith. As a blacksmith is a metalsmith who creates objects from wrought iron or steel by forging the metal, you should be a skilled user of words. A wordsmith is one who hears and keeps to the words of God.

1. "Do not deceive yourselves by just listening to his word; instead, put it into practice" (James 1:22 Good News Translation).

MEDITATION FOR THE DAY:

HOLY SPIRIT, HELP ME TO BE A DOER OF YOUR WORDS. LET EVERY WORD YOU HAVE SPOKEN ABOUT ME COME TO PASS.

January 19: Another Helper

Life is challenging. The demands of family, career, business, ministry, relationships, and the quest to find purpose can be daunting. We cannot achieve meaningful goals without the help of others and most especially without the help of the Holy Spirit.

1. "Then I will ask the Father to send you the Holy Spirit who will help you and always be with you."
   (John 14:16 Contemporary English Version)

Why do we need the Holy Spirit? As humans, we fail sometimes. We have our struggles and challenges that keep us thinking about ourselves alone.

But the Holy Spirit is always there to help you, be with you, and take you to the next level.

MEDITATION FOR THE DAY:

HOLY SPIRIT, I ACKNOWLEDGE YOU AS MY HELPER IN LIFE, IN JESUS' NAME!

January 20: He will Guide

We are living in an era where there are so many distractions. We are being presented with multiple paths and choices that either take us further from what is true or keep us grappling for what we have always known to be the truth.

1. "The Spirit shows what is true and will come and guide you into the full truth." (John 14:16 Contemporary English Version)

The truths about your life, your purpose, your destiny, and how you should live while still on earth are in the Holy Spirit. You have never been or lived on earth before. He executed the creation plan of the Godhead.

He is the only one that can truly guide you. acknowledge Him, seek to know Him, and walk with Him daily.

MEDITATION FOR THE DAY:

HOLY SPIRIT, YOU KNOW ALL TRUTHS, GUIDE MY PATH IN ALL MY ENDEAVORS, IN JESUS' NAME!

January 21: He will Show

There are so many things we do not know and understand. And there are many things you and I may struggle with for a long time if we don't know what to do. God has a way out of all our life's issues. The Holy Spirit can show you what to do.

1. "...he will show you things to come." (John 16:13 King James 2000 Bible)

The Holy Spirit has the benefit of hindsight, insight, and foresight. The things you and I can never know or understand, the Holy Spirit can show us with ease, as we genuinely love, acknowledge, and walk with Him.

"Ask me, and I will tell you things that you don't know and can't find out." (Jeremiah 33:3 CEV)

MEDITATION FOR THE DAY:

HOLY SPIRIT, I OPEN MY HEART TO YOU, SHOW ME WHAT TO DO IN ALL MY ENDEAVORS, IN JESUS' NAME!

January 22: He will bring

Every one of us deals with the issue of forgetfulness and retaining information every other time. But some of us consistently have memory blocks and struggle to recall or remember important information when we most need them.

1. "The Helper, the Holy Spirit... will... make you remember all..." (John 14:26 GNT)

Memory problems such as transience, absentmindedness, blocking, bias, or forgetfulness can be healed when our lives are animated and controlled by the Holy Spirit.

You may be in an examination environment, a strategic business meeting, or even a heated argument, and the Holy Spirit can bring the information you need to remembrance.

MEDITATION FOR THE DAY:

HOLY SPIRIT, I YIELD MY MIND TO YOUR CONTROL, IN JESUS' NAME!

January 23: He will Teach

We are living in an age driven by information and a hunger for knowledge. We are eager to know what is in trend, which unconsciously opens us up to strange beliefs that are harmful to us – our future, relationships, and our walk with God.

1. "The Helper, the Holy Spirit, whom the Father will send in my name, will teach you everything …" (John 14:26 GNT)

God has hidden all the treasures of wisdom and knowledge in Christ (Colossians 2:3. GWT). When we seek teachings and help from other sources, to resolve the issues of our lives, they will only lead us to a deeper mess.

The Holy Spirit wants to teach you everything you need to succeed in life. Please trust and depend on Him

MEDITATION FOR THE DAY:

HOLY SPIRIT, YOU'RE MY TEACHER. I DEPEND ON YOU, IN JESUS' NAME!

January 24: He will Represent

The power of referral or the person (s) you know, cannot be underestimated when it comes to closing business deals or establishing strategic relationships. I struggled to make a break in business until a loved one put in a word for me with a major enterprise development player. The rest is history.

1. "But when the Father sends the Advocate as my representative—that is, the Holy Spirit…" (John 14:26 NLT)

What do you do when you do not have anyone to refer you? Do you resolve to the fate that you do not know anyone?

The Holy Spirit is in and with you. He turns situations in the favor of those who walk with Him. He is your Advocate!

MEDITATION FOR THE DAY:

HOLY SPIRIT, YOU'RE MY ADVOCATE, THANK YOU FOR SPEAKING ON MY BEHALF, IN JESUS' NAME!

January 25: He will Counsel

To find a genuine, perfect, and experienced counselor, who can completely help you resolve all your problems is a tall order. Most advice we get is short-lived – because whomever we seek counsel from is also seeking one.

1. "But the Counselor, the Holy Spirit, whom the Father will send in my name, he will teach you all things…" (John 14:26 World English Bible)

Our human counselors can only counsel us in an area that they have had experience with or are educated about. But the Holy Spirit provides counsel in all life's matters. No human problems are beyond His resolution.

Love Him, seek Him, walk with Him, and you will have unlimited access to His counsel on any issue of life!

MEDITATION FOR THE DAY:

HOLY SPIRIT, YOU'RE MY COUNSELOR. I RECEIVE YOUR ADVICE IN ALL LIFE'S ISSUES, IN JESUS' NAME!

January 26: He's with You

The pressures, demands, and activities of life have a way of making you feel that no one cares about you. The pull from all angles – work, business, family, friends, and society leave you empty and dry.

1. "Then I will ask the Father to send you the Holy Spirit who will help you and always be with you" (John 14:16 Contemporary English Version)

As long as we still live on earth, we cannot escape the stress, pressures, and demands of others. Your source of strength and hope is in the Holy Spirit. He is here to help you with the weight of our human burdens, and He will always be with you.

MEDITATION FOR THE DAY:

HOLY SPIRIT, I RECEIVE YOUR STRENGTH AND COMFORT, IN JESUS' NAME!

January 27: He's the Truth

Everyone seeks the truth. Things are happening in our lives that make us want to know the reasons behind our challenges and predicaments. This has led many of us to seek the help of mediums, seers, prophets, and occult powers. But the answers we get or seek are far from what we expect.

1. "When the Holy Spirit, who is truth, comes, he shall guide you into all truth, for he will not be presenting his own ideas, but will be passing on to you what he has heard. He will tell you about the future." (John 16:13 TLB)

The truth you seek is in the Holy Spirit. Ask Him about your past, your present, and your future.

He knows all the truth. Ask Him to take the lead in your life now!

MEDITATION FOR THE DAY:

HOLY SPIRIT, REVEAL MY PAST, PRESENT, AND FUTURE TO ME, IN JESUS' NAME!

January 28: He will Empower

The Holy Spirit is a person. He has been given the authority to govern the affairs of those who believe in Jesus and to demonstrate the abilities of God in all areas of their lives. His fruit (Galatians 5:22-23) and His gifts (1 Corinthians 12:4-11) have been given to you, to empower you to live a life of dominion. The Holy Spirit wants to help you - do not run your life feeling helpless:

1. "I will ask the Father, and he will give you another helper who will be with you forever." (John 14:16 16 GWT)

MEDITATION FOR THE DAY:

HOLY SPIRIT, I RECEIVE THE FULLNESS OF YOUR FRUIT TO LIVE THE LIFE YOU HAVE ORDAINED FOR ME, I RECEIVE YOUR GIFTS TO BE A BLESSING TO MY FAMILY, OTHERS, AND THE WORLD.

January 29: Be Spiritually Empowered

Everyone seeks the truth. Things are happening in life that make us want to know the reasons behind our challenges and predicaments. This has led many of us to seek the help of mediums, seers, prophets, and occult powers. But the answers we get or seek are far from what we expect.

1. "When the Holy Spirit, who is truth, comes, he shall guide you into all truth, for he will not be presenting his own ideas, but will be passing on to you what he has heard. He will tell you about the future." (John 16:13 TLB)

The truth you seek is in the Holy Spirit. Ask Him about your past, your present, and your future.

He knows all the truth. Ask Him to take the lead in your life now!

MEDITATION FOR THE DAY:

HOLY SPIRIT, REVEAL MY PAST, PRESENT & FUTURE TO ME, IN JESUS' NAME!

January 30: Live Instructively

The beauty and dangers of liberty come with our willingness to follow instructions. If there is one flaw about humanity – we hate to live by rules, laws, and order. We dislike boundaries and see others who obey instructions as being weak or timid.

1. "Listen carefully to my instructions, and you will be wise." (Proverbs 8:33 Contemporary English Version)

God has given us rules to live by in our relationships with others, marriage, work, leadership, finances, health, and many other areas of life. But we will rather give excuses for taking a different path that always leads to pain, shame, and regrets.

The results you see in life are the outcomes of the instructions you obey.

Live instructively!

MEDITATION FOR THE DAY:

HOLY SPIRIT, HELP ME TO YIELD TO YOUR LIFE-CHANGING INSTRUCTIONS, IN JESUS' NAME!

January 31: An Empowered Life

Life is filled with arrays of battles! We are constantly engaged in spiritual, emotional, physical, mental, and financial battles. we need cutting-edge strategies; we need to tap into the resources that have been made available to us:

1. "Put on all the armor that God supplies. In this way you can take a stand against the devil's strategies." (Ephesians 6:11 GWT)

You have been empowered to reign in life. God has given you access to an unlimited supply of strategies in His Word – the BIBLE, to overcome every challenge you will ever encounter.

Leverage on it – YOU ARE EMPOWERED!

MEDITATION FOR THE DAY:

HOLY SPIRIT, THANK YOU FOR BEING MY SOURCE OF EMPOWERMENT, IN JESUS' NAME!

February 1: Made for More

The value of a product is unlocked as the manufacturer's manual is used appropriately. The value of your life is unlocked as you:

1. Use your manufacturer's manual – the bible by diligently studying and meditating on the truths of what God has said about you
2. Believe and consciously keep speaking the truths God has said about you

My life has experienced amazing kindness, healing, love, and renewal from God in the last three (3) years as I relied on the Holy Spirit to study, meditate, believe, and speak what God says about me.

You are not ordinary! The forces of life and the challenges you are going through are raging to bring out the best of the sweet fragrance in your life.

YOU ARE MADE FOR MORE!

MEDITATION FOR THE DAY:

I AM MADE FOR MORE; MY TRUE VALUE IS IN WHAT GOD SAYS ABOUT ME!

February 2: Unbreakable

Do you ever wonder how you went through those nights, days, and moments of tears, pains, uncertainty, hopelessness, disappointments, and unrealized dreams?

1. God framed your soul, spirit, and body to withstand the pressures of life (whether caused by our errors or by circumstances outside our control)

2. God uses everything – I mean everything that happens to you to shape your life, your dreams, and your future.

Family, relationships, career, business, financial challenges - even death can never break you. No force on earth can break you except YOU!

Your sweet Fragrance is released to our world as you remain UNBREAKABLE in the face of life's adversities. Scriptures: Romans 8:28-30, 37-39

MEDITATION FOR THE DAY:

I AM UNBREAKABLE, I RISE ABOVE THE CHALLENGES OF LIFE!

February 3: Unstoppable

The path to dream fulfillment and greatness comes with favor, envy, hatred, failures, trials, disappointments, and self-doubts. How did Joseph in the bible survive? How did I go through the pain of death and still hope for the future? How will you become unstoppable?

1. Keep your heart and eyes on the big picture of what the bible says and what God's specific word(s) to you

2. Depend on the Holy Spirit and build healthy relationships that will provide support through your seasons of fears, self-doubt, and uncertainty.

As mortals cannot stop the force of a tsunami, life cannot stop you from becoming all God has destined you to be – YOU'RE UNSTOPPABLE!

MEDITATION FOR THE DAY:

I AM UNSTOPPABLE, GREATNESS IS IN ME!

February 4: Unconquerable

One secret I wish for is to go through this world without worries, struggles, or battles. With over four decades on earth, that wish has not been granted. What then makes us unconquerable in the fiercest battles of life?

1. The victory God has already given to you in Jesus Christ (make Him your Lord and Savior).
2. The tremendous LIFE-CHANGING power in the spoken and written word of God to bring to reality the victory God has given to you.

The battles of sickness, diseases, heartbreaks, failures, disappointments, bankruptcy, persecution, divorce, and even death will rage.

But God has given you an OVERWHELMING VICTORY IN CHRIST because – YOU'RE UNCONQUERABLE!

MEDITATION FOR THE DAY:

I HAVE AN OVERWHELMING VICTORY IN CHRIST JESUS!

February 5: Immovable

The successes of great men and women ignite the potential in me to achieve greatness. The depth of criticism, bad-mouthing, and intense challenges that comes with being great, makes me rethink sometimes. The amazing thing is that successful people are not moved by what people say and the challenges they face. How can you remain undistracted?

1. Stay focused on the big picture (vision, mission, assignment, passion, and calling) God has given to you.
2. Make a conscious choice to excel in your work by doing your best (like a tree by the waterside, you will flourish amidst human draught).

Our world is filled with wickedness, distractions, and challenges, and only those who refuse to pay attention to the noises make the best out of their lives.

MEDITATION FOR THE DAY:

GREATNESS IS IN ME; I'M IMMOVABLE!

February 6: Unshakable

I listened to a great preacher (late Arch. Bishop Benson Idahosa) who said that a fish will not jump out of the sea to live on land because the waves are too heavy, and neither will a horse rider jump off a horse because the horse gallops. You cannot give in to life's adversities because of the pressures. You will be unshakable when you:

1. Engage in fervent prayers with thanksgiving knowing that your victory is guaranteed in Jesus Christ.
2. Seek the help of the Holy Spirit to go through the adversities with joy and believe that you will come out better and stronger.

If we faint in moments of adversity, our strength is small.

Hold on to God, declare your victory in Jesus, depend on the Holy Spirit and connect with people that can uphold you through the challenges.

MEDITATION FOR THE DAY:

VICTORY IS MINE IN ALL CIRCUMSTANCES!

February 7: Indestructible

The hold of fear in our lives when faced with challenges, sometimes cripples us. We become afraid of the things we should not be afraid of. Jesus (Matt. 10:28) gave us the clue to master the outcomes of any situation in our lives:

1. You cannot be afraid of those or anything that can kill your body.
2. You cannot be afraid of those or anything that can kill your soul (the state of your SPIRIT matters most during life's challenges).

"Don't be bluffed into silence by the threats of bullies (the challenges you're facing – they are just bullies). There is nothing they can do to your soul, your core being. Save your fear for God, who holds your entire life—body and soul—in his hands" (MSG).

No matter what you will go through or going through now - you're indestructible!

MEDITATION FOR THE DAY:

I AM INDESTRUCTIBLE, I'M BUILT TO LAST!

February 8: Built to Last

All things made on the earth have an expiry date. One thing is made to outlast this world – YOU (your human spirit). When you face the challenges of life, live in the consciousness of these facts that your human spirit cannot be broken and:

1. No life's struggles, failures, sorrows, pains, and hurts can overcome you.
2. Your construction composition is made of God's breath (that last into eternity – life after now).

Your physical body will not last forever, but the real you have been designed to outlast all circumstances on earth.

You have what it takes to overcome that situation and dominate it. YOU WERE BUILT TO LAST!

MEDITATION FOR THE DAY:

I AM BUILT TO LAST, I'M NOT A VICTIM BUT A VICTORY!

February 9: Thoughts Replacement

It is so easy to have thoughts of fear, impossibility, uncertainty, and negativity. Most scary is speaking of them as our reality. No one thinks and speaks negatively, and yet expects to SEE positive outcomes in his or her life. These three disciplines will keep you on God's frequency for your thought replacement:

1. Discipline your thoughts to think about what God thinks about your issues.
2. Discipline your words to speak what God says about your situation.
3. Discipline your actions to act in line with God's thoughts and God's words.

I am experiencing an amazing shift through deliberate thought-replacement.

Your life will experience the shift you need as you REPLACE YOUR THOUGHTS WITH GOD'S (The bible)!

MEDITATION FOR THE DAY:

I THINK FAITH-FILLED THOUGHTS, I SPEAK FAITH-FILLED WORDS!

February 10: Milestone Prayer

Challenges are surmountable as you engage in prayers with the name of Jesus, God's words, and your bold statements. You will HAVE what you SAY. I declare:

- I am made for more; my true value is in what god says about me. I am unbreakable!
- I rise above the challenges of life. I am unstoppable, greatness is in me!
- I have an overwhelming victory in Christ Jesus! Greatness is in me!
- I'm immovable! Victory is mine in all circumstances!
- I am indestructible, I'm built to last. I am built to last, I'm not a victim but a victor!

MEDITATION FOR THE DAY:

I THINK FAITH-FILLED THOUGHTS, I SPEAK FAITH-FILLED WORDS!

February 11: Immutability of God (1)

It is impossible for God to change who He is because of what we go through. He is unchanging in His character, will, and covenant promises. He craves a relationship with you that can be experienced every day as you:

1. SHARE your thoughts and feelings with Him- be open, bare, and unscripted.
2. TRUST and obey His guidance, instructions, and principles.

You can pour out your heart and discuss any issues of your life with Him – His perspectives are life-changing.

Humans will change, and we will disappoint and break each other's hearts, but God remains IMMUTABLE and longs for you...

MEDITATION FOR THE DAY:

MY FATHER AND GOD, KEEP MY HEART FOCUSED ON YOU, IN THE MIDST OF LIFE-CHANGING SITUATIONS.

February 12: Immutability of God (2)

Life's changing situations cannot be stopped. Getting married, giving birth, changing careers, broken dreams, broken hearts, pains – even death will be regular occurrences in this world (I have had my share of these). Do not give up on God but:

1. LEARN to care about what God cares about (YOU, others & His purposes.)
2. DESIRE God's friendship more than anything else.

Friendship with God gives you strength through changing seasons in life. "Hear His words, act on them, and you will be like the far-sighted, practical, and sensible individual who built on a strong foundation".

God is IMMUTABLE (unchanging)!

MEDITATION FOR THE DAY:

MY FATHER AND GOD, YOU'RE MY STRENGTH LIKE NO OTHER!

February 13: Do not Give Up

I have been in situations that drained me and made me helpless and hopeless. No strength in me to go on. We are faced with circumstances that snuff out the joy and hope of living, and all we think at those moments is: "I GIVE UP". "I'M FED UP".

1. You cannot give up! Challenges are designed to make you and not break you.
2. Whatever you go through is proof of your "being" and your process of becoming a beacon of hope to others.

We live in a broken and sin-FULL world. Our joy is that we have an IMMUTABLE (unchanging) God who through His son Jesus Christ, makes you & I victorious in all we go through.

Don't GIVE UP, instead, GIVE IN TO JESUS.

MEDITATION FOR THE DAY:

IN CHRIST, I AM VICTORIOUS IN ALL ISSUES OF LIFE!

February 14: Love Notes

No other book truly reveals how love is intended to rule in our hearts and lives, except the BIBLE. Please read below, some of God's notes to you this valentine's day:

1. I have loved you with an everlasting love (unconditionally) – Jeremiah 31:2
2. I love you so much and care about all your needs – 1 Peter 5:7
3. I love you and desire that you be healthy and prosperous in all you do – 3 John 2
4. I love you so much not to leave you hopeless – Hebrew 13:5
5. My love does not cause you to fear – 1 John 4:18

I love you so much and proved it through the death of my precious son -Jesus (in Him resides all that you need to succeed in life) – John 3:16, 1 John 3:16 & 18

MEDITATION FOR THE DAY:

GOD LOVES ME; THAT'S ALL THAT MATTERS.

February 15: Love Drained?

'Love never fails, it never fades nor ends. But I have seen how it gets drained when consistently abused and taken advantage of despite all you do to be loved in return. How can you keep yourself sane during the love-draining cycle?

1. Pour your heart completely into God. He fixes drained hearts and brings unimaginable beauty.

2. Love YOU unconditionally. Get involved in healthy and godly leisure activities that make you happy such as traveling, learning new things, volunteering, and rediscovering YOU!

Love is propelled by sacrifice and strengthened when appreciated. Are you feeling drained from giving love? Do you feel loveless?

Be encouraged, you have God's kind of heart. His healing and restoration are a sure bet as you pour your heart into Him.

MEDITATION FOR THE DAY:

LORD, HEAL MY HEART, WRAP ME IN YOUR ENDLESS LOVE.

February 16: Self-Worth (1)

I grew up with low self-esteem and timidness. I had a poor self-image until my 2nd year in college (university). I gave in easily to things, was afraid to stand up for myself and others, and wished I was like others. What changed all of these?

1. I discovered and still discovering who God says I am as I invest time in reading the bible – Genesis to Revelation (for almost two decades now and still counting).

2. My contact and relationship with people who have a healthy self-image of their personality (one of my former bosses comes to mind 😊)

Your self-worth comes from God's word. You are in the class of royalty.

Jesus' death on the cross affirms the importance of YOUR SELF-WORTH! Believe in Him.

MEDITATION FOR THE DAY:

I AM WORTH THE WORLD TO GOD!

February 17: Self-Worth (2)

Your self-worth determines how you see and respond to situations. The way you relate with people and how you handle life's challenges. You can have increasing self-worth as you:

1. Develop your spiritual, mental, emotional, physical, and financial capacities.
2. Cultivate healthy relationships and networks that add value to your self-confidence and net worth.

You may have gone through trials that made you feel so little about yourself. Low self-esteem keeps people under, and it is one of the devil's strategies to kill your dreams and purpose.

You are made in God's image, see YOU the way God sees you!

MEDITATION FOR THE DAY:

I AM WHO GOD SAYS I AM – MADE IN HIS IMAGE!

February 18: Change Me

I woke up one morning angry because I was yet to get a response from individuals, I trusted them to support my career path. The Holy Spirit whispered to me "they may be going through their issues" and took me through this process of:

1. Praying for them that God will meet them at the point of their needs.
2. Casting my concerns about the expectations from them to God.

You and I cannot change people or situations most of the time to meet our expectations.

But we can change the state of our hearts by praying about it and turning our hearts to God who alone can change people and situations.

MEDITATION FOR THE DAY:

CHANGE ME O GOD, MAKE ME MORE LIKE YOU.

February 19: Be Strengthened

Our mastery over life's challenges is displayed during times of pressure and trials. David (in the bible) was greatly distressed and was going to be stoned to death during a crucial moment in his life. David showed us two secrets to victory in life:

1. He felt strengthened and encouraged in the Lord His God.
2. He asked God what steps to take and what the outcomes will be.

The rest we say is history. We must develop the discipline to encourage ourselves in God, put our trust in His words during trials (He can take care of anything), but most importantly ask Him: "what will you have me do?" (God knows the way out).

Trials will come but "the people who know their God will display strength and take action (to resist)."

MEDITATION FOR THE DAY:

I AM STRENGTHENED IN GOD, VICTORY IS MINE!

February 20: Prayer for You

"When two of you get together on anything at all on earth and make a prayer of it, my Father in heaven goes into action". In faith with you, I pray and declare:

- God will keep your heart focused on Him, during life's changing situations.
- God shall be your strength like no other.
- In Christ, you're victorious in all issues of life.
- God heals your heart and wraps you in His endless love.
- You're worth the world to God. Hallelujah!
- You're whom God says you're – made in His image.
- You're changed by the power of God and becoming more like Him.

MEDITATION FOR THE DAY:

I AM STRENGTHENED IN GOD AND VICTORY IS MINE!

February 21: Waiting

The word "wait", is one word our prayers cannot take out of the dictionary. Living in a generation where everything works at the speed of lightning makes it more frustrating why we must wait to receive answers to our prayers.

1. Waiting builds your faith and shapes your character (many of us are not ready for the outcomes of our prayers. God prepares us in our moments of waiting.
2. Waiting brings God's perspective and foreknowledge in taking care of obstacles we may encounter at the end of the tunnel.

The meeting of your desires is secretly tied to the principle of seed and harvest time – your expectations go through different processes which you and I cannot see with our physical eyes.

Waiting can be unpleasant, but it brings out the best in YOU!

MEDITATION FOR THE DAY: O LORD, TEACH ME THE PATIENCE OF WAITING ON YOU.

February 22: Waiting - How Long?

The "How long" question is an aged-long one. A great king once poured out his heart to God: "How long, Lord? Will you forget me forever? How long will you hide your face from me? How long must I wrestle with my thoughts and day after day have sorrow in my heart?"

1. What you are waiting on God for, has been overcome by another. The temptations in your life are no different from what others experience.

2. What God has done for one, He can do much more for another (for YOU)!

How long you wait is God's prerogative (all things being equal) if you and I do not take the shortcut.

What you do while waiting to see the reality of your expectations matters. Do not short-circuit God's process - WAIT!

MEDITATION FOR THE DAY: MY FATHER, I TRUST WHAT YOU ARE DOING BEHIND THE SCENES.

February 23: Delay, Not Denial

I have heard so much and come to believe that: "Life is not a sprint but a marathon." Our soul dislikes the idea of delays. Delays happen at God's knowledge of your situation and the enemies' plot to hurt you:

1. Yet God has made everything beautiful for its own time (Eccl. 3:11 - NLT). The delays you are experiencing have an end date
2. For the enemy shall come like a flood, but the Spirit of the Lord shall chase him away (Isaiah 59:19 - GNV)

Experiencing delays in a traffic situation does not hinder us from getting to our destination. Through slow and steady movement, you will always arrive at your place of joy.

God does not arrive late, and delays to His promises do not mean His denial – WAIT!

MEDITATION FOR THE DAY:

JESUS, I BELIEVE IN YOUR PROMISES, I WILL WAIT ON YOU!

February 24: God is Not in a Hurry

I recall when I was waiting on God for a child. I heard a statement that has not left me (even after the fulfillment of my desire): "There's nothing you can do, no prayer you can offer that will make me send a child to the world when it's not yet time."

1. God has planned how your life will turn out. He is not in a hurry to alter it except you make the process longer by taking a short-cut.

2. Develop your heart (spirit) to know His thoughts concerning what you are waiting on Him for. His response will give you priceless reassurance.

Imagine God's thoughts: "At the time I have decided, my words will come true. You can trust what I say about the future. It may take a long time but keep on waiting— it will happen!" (Habakkuk 2:3 CEV). WAIT, GOD IS NOT IN A HURRY!

MEDITATION FOR THE DAY: MY GOD, LET YOUR WORDS COME TRUE AT THE TIME YOU HAVE DECIDED.

February 25: Why Me?

Why me? When we ask this question during our difficult moments in life, we either seek to know the reason behind our sufferings and pains or what God is working on behind the scenes through the stressful and pressure-filled moments. Few lessons through mine:

1. God moves in a mysterious way… a way that only a few of us will have access to as we draw closer to Him.
2. His purposes will ripen fast, unfolding every hour. The bud may have a bitter taste, but sweet will be the flower.

There are questions we may not get answers to in our life until we get to heaven. Why you? You are the only one apportioned to go through what you are going through – and the grace to ride through the storms of it.

Why you? WAIT!

MEDITATION FOR THE DAY: I WILL HOPE IN GOD AND WAIT EXPECTANTLY FOR HIM. (Psalms 42:5,11 Amplified)

February 26: Stay Calm, Engage

What we do, and how we respond or react during our challenges proves our maturity and eventually the outcome. We cannot experience tangible growth lessons learned when all we do is fear, doubt, complain, transfer blame, and ask why me?

1. People with their minds set on God, He keeps completely whole, and steady on their feet, because they keep at it and do not quit.
2. You must depend on God and keep at it because in the Lord God you have a sure thing (Isaiah 26:3 MSG)

Engaging daily with the Bible through praying, reading, studying, meditating, doing, and saying what God says, empowers you over life's issues. We become weak when we are anxious and far from God's word.

Wait for Him and you shall not be moved!

MEDITATION FOR THE DAY:

I WILL STAY CALM; MY TRUST IS IN GOD!

February 27: Re-Location

In 2009, I was in a very frustrating place in my life. I was 'broke' (no money in my pocket or bank account), stressed, and under great pressure. Things were not working out for me as I had thought. I made up my mind to relocate to another city for a change until a mentor I cherish said to me:

1. 'Joe-man', relocating from one city to another city will not change the process you are going through.
2. Your relocation will only lengthen the process of development you are meant to learn in this season of your life

Those words sounded like the worst advice you can give to someone going through lack and desperation. I am thankful to God that I did not relocate.

What you might be going through will not be solved through relocation but by waiting and trusting in God!

MEDITATION FOR THE DAY: O LORD, I WILL WAIT UNTIL MY CHANGE COMES!

February 28: Praise Break

What a marvelous God we serve! He has given us another wonderful day - the last one in the month of February, a day you and I will never see again. Please:

1. Take a break from focusing on all that is going on around you and just praise God for who He is - HE IS GOD ALL BY HIMSELF!
2. Take a praise break! Everything is in His control - your life and your worries.

Give God all your attention today, let Him fill your thoughts and heart. Praise and thanksgiving are amazing spiritual mysteries that unlock His presence in your life. His presence even causes mountains to skip like rams!

Take a praise break today!

MEDITATION FOR THE DAY:

PRAISE IS ALL I WILL DO, NO MATTER WHAT I'M GOING THROUGH!

February 29: Another Leap Year!

We have leap years because the seasons and astronomical events don't repeat in whole numbers. In a solar year, the length of time it takes the Earth to travel around the sun is 365.25 days. We have a leap year every four years so that it can catch up to the solar year. Overall, it's important to have a leap year so our calendars don't get mixed up. (https://www.entitymag.com/what-is-a-leap-year/)

1. Every leap year should remind us of the wonders and creation of God.
2. A leap year gives many of us every four years the opportunity to celebrate a special day in our lives.

No matter what day it is, my hope and prayers are that you will take one more leap to actualize your dreams and aspirations.

MEDITATION FOR THE DAY:

EVERY DAY IS A DAY CLOSER TO THE FULFILLMENT OF MY DREAMS!

March 1: 31 days Challenge

How come the number of days, weeks, and months run so fast? There is so much we want to achieve but so few results to show; time never really waits for our challenges, excuses, and self-pity. As we approach the end of the first quarter of each year:

1. Where do you feel so limited? Career, relationship, academics, work, business? Where are you Spiritually, Emotionally, Mentally, Physically, and financially?

2. What do you plan to do about these areas of your life that make you feel so weak, powerless, and unfulfilled?

God has given us the ability to make progress in life through the help of the Holy Spirit. You can pray, meditate on God's word, read a book, change a habit, hang around great people, serve others, and enroll in a course.

I challenge you this month – make the next 31 days count and be remarkable for YOU!

MEDITATION FOR THE DAY: I MAKE PROGRESS THIS MONTH THROUGH CHRIST JESUS!

March 2:   Prayer for You

We win the battles of life by putting our faith in God's truth. "They won the victory over him by the blood of the Lamb and by the truth which they proclaimed" (Rev. 12:11 GNT). Let us proclaim these truths with prayers of faith:

- Lord teach me the patience of waiting on you!
- My Father, I trust what you are doing behind the scenes. It is for my good.
- Jesus, I believe in your promises, I will wait on you!
- My God, let your words come true at the time you have decided! Your timing is right for me.
- I will hope in God and wait expectantly for Him. My expectations will not be cut short
- I will stay calm; my trust is in God!
- Lord, I will wait until my change comes!

MEDITATION FOR THE DAY:

PRAISE IS ALL I WILL DO, NO MATTER WHAT I'M GOING THROUGH!

March 3: Spirit-Being

One of the greatest mysteries of all time is YOU! The thoughts, purpose, and composition behind your existence baffle the whole of creation. Even the barred lead singer in heaven still wonders why God created and loves you so much:

1. You are someone like the Godhead, created to be the master of all life upon the earth and in the skies and in the seas (Genesis 1:26 TLB)
2. You are more than what you think about yourself now – YOU'RE A SPIRIT BEING!

You are not like any other creation of God. I learned early in my walk with God that I have and reflect the nature of the Godhead (Genesis 1:26 MSG)!

Until you know who you are, life can be a roller coaster. You are a spirit being, reflecting God's nature.

MEDITATION FOR THE DAY:

I KNOW WHO I AM, I HAVE GOD'S NATURE IN ME!

March 4: Fearfully Made

Have you thought about what it means to be fearfully made? That amidst our self-pity, self-condemnation, limitations, struggles, and challenges, God still sees us as being fearfully made? How could this be?

1. You are the only creation the Godhead made a conscious decision to be the master of all life upon the earth and in the skies and in the seas.
2. You are the only creation that has the Spirit of God – functioning with a higher level of knowledge, insight, and authority.

These are a few of the many fearful reasons that define who you are. God amazingly made you to be feared by the challenges of life.

Do not live life being fearful. You were created to have dominion and not to be dominated!

MEDITATION FOR THE DAY:

I AM AN AMAZING CREATION OF GOD!

March 5:   Wonderfully Made

The beauty of creation brings joy to the human heart but the making of human life remains a wonder! Science has tried to give us vivid descriptions of the birth process. Read what God says before science could talk about the existence of the fetus:

1. Before I started to put you together with your mother, I knew you before you were born (Jeremiah 1:5 New Life Version)
2. You have unique spiritual gifts, heart desires, abilities, personality, and experience no one has – an amazing wonder of YOU!

This devotional is not enough to capture your wonder of you. From the tip of your hair, the color of your eyes, the shape of your lips, your body, your heartbeat, your biometrics… Oh my God!

Do not let the issues of life steal the WONDER OF YOU!

MEDITATION FOR THE DAY:

I AM FEARFULLY AND WONDERFULLY MADE IN GOD!

March 6: Who Am I?

Truly, God has fearfully and wonderfully made us. But it is so burdensome that one of the greatest struggles that drain us during life's battles is "Identity Crisis". Many of us define our lives by our experiences. I was a shadow of myself when I had a major loss in my life.

1. Your identity in life is in God. If nothing in the universe can stop God, whatever you are going through or will ever go through, cannot stop you!

The negative outcome of a relationship does not define you. A failed business or examination, delayed aspirations, or an uncertain career path are all part of your success stories. Do you want to know who you are?

You are created in the class of the Godhead to be the master of all life upon the earth and in the skies and in the seas (Genesis 1:26 TLB)

MEDITATION FOR THE DAY: I AM WHO GOD SAYS I AM -A MASTER OF LIFE UPON THE EARTH!

March 7:   In-Formation

The intake of what we see, hear, and experience is a key resource or material that forms the foundation of what we become in life. We are a sum of what we consistently see, hear, think, and speak about. And our heart or mind is the seat where this formation takes place. Hence:

1. You'll do best by filling your minds and meditating on things true, noble, reputable, authentic, compelling, gracious—the best, not the worst; the beautiful, not the ugly; things to praise, not things to curse (Phil. 4:8 MSG)

The mastery of life is in the depth of information that enters our hearts. Whatever enters your heart – enters your life! Gratefully, God has given us the greatest bank of information in life – The Bible.

Study it and see unprecedented results!

MEDITATION FOR THE DAY: MY LIFE'S REALITY IS INFORMED BY GOD'S WORD!

March 8: Small in Strength

Every conflict in life challenges the character, maturity, aspirations, strengths, and weaknesses we have built over time. When the storms of life surge with intensity, it tests the stuff we are made up of. How you perform reveals who you are!

1. Consider it a sheer gift, friends, when tests and challenges come at you from all sides. You know that under pressure, your faith life is forced into the open and shows its true colors (James 1:2 MSG)

Will you feel beaten? Yes! Will you be disappointed, heartbroken, and hurt? Why not! Will you feel like giving up or throwing in the towel? The mighty and successful are caught up in this too. But you MUST not stay down and out because, "If you fall to pieces in a crisis, there wasn't much to you in the first place (Proverbs 24:10 MSG)".

There is much to you and God - the Greater One lives in YOU!

MEDITATION FOR THE DAY: I HAVE THE VICTORY IN (call the issues) IN CHRIST JESUS!

March 9: Anchor

An anchor is a device, normally made of metal, used to connect a vessel to the bed of a body of water to prevent the craft from drifting due to wind or current. The word comes from the Greek (ankura). It can either be temporary or permanent (Wikipedia).

1. Where do you anchor your life to prevent you from drifting when the wind and current of life come your path?

Here are the lyrics of a song (Cornerstone – Hillsong): "When darkness seems to hide His face, I rest on His unchanging grace, in every high and stormy gale, my anchor holds within the veil. Christ alone, Cornerstone, weak made strong in the Savior's love, Through the storm, He is Lord, Lord of all."

Let Christ alone, be your cornerstone and anchor in and for all seasons of your life! He is the only permanent anchor ever.

MEDITATION FOR THE DAY:

JESUS IS MY ANCHOR IN THE MIDST OF LIFE'S STORMS!

March 10: Act

As humans, we have made so much advancement because of our ability to take bold steps and actions to actualize our progress and dreams. But I discover one area of life we struggle with is, acting on what God says. Yet, God says:

1. This command I give you today is not too hard for you. It is not beyond what you can do (Deuteronomy 30:11 ICB)
2. The word that saves is right here, as near as the tongue in your mouth, as close as the heart in your chest (Romans 10:8 MSG)

Acting upon the word of God can be hard, but also the easiest and priceless solution to our problems and challenges. It is convenient to believe in the existence of God, yet difficult to believe in what He has asked us to act on, for example: "be anxious for nothing".

MEDITATION FOR THE DAY:

LORD JESUS, HELP MY STRUGGLES WITH ACTING ON YOUR WORD.

March 11: Just Do It

A great brand's slogan (Nike) that resonated and propelled me over time is "Just do it"! It also recalls Mary – the mother of Jesus' instruction to some servants "Whatever he tells you, do it" in solving wine shortage at a wedding ceremony. (John 2:5)

1. Whatever God says – Just do it. Your blessing is in obedience. If you are willing and obedient, you shall eat the good of the land (Isaiah 1:19 ESV)
2. The reason why God sent the Holy Spirit is to help you do what God says with ease. Let Him help you. You will always have struggles in your heart.

How can we handle what God says? JUST DO WHAT HE SAYS! We cannot always figure out how things and processes should work. God's process of bringing to pass our desires is in obedience.

JUST DO IT!

MEDITATION FOR THE DAY:

I RECEIVE THE GRACE TO DO WHAT GOD SAYS IN JESUS' NAME!

March 12:   Prayer for You

Today, as we take time out to pray for ourselves, I want us to remember the people who have lost their lives in different disasters - plane crashes, floods, famine, wars, accidents, and pandemic. May their souls rest in peace. Amen!

- Heavenly Father, we pray for comfort for the families of those who have lost their loved ones.
- Give us the grace to find meaning and purpose in life for your glory.
- I am fearfully and wonderfully made to glorify God.
- I am who God says I am – a master of life upon the earth.
- My life's reality is informed by God's word.
- Jesus is my anchor amid life's storms.
- Lord Jesus, help my struggles with acting on your word.

MEDITATION FOR THE DAY:

I RECEIVE THE GRACE TO DO WHAT GOD SAYS IN JESUS' NAME!

March 13:   Force of Pain (1)

Experiencing pain is one aspect of life that brings discomfort and agony to our hearts. The loss of loved ones – child, spouse, parent, sibling, friend, etc. Also, encountering ghastly accidents, disappointments, failures, and heartbreaks in different areas of life can be excruciating. What do you do in moments like this?

1.   Never isolate yourself. These moments can be the most vulnerable season of your life. Open your heart to God, a sincere-caring family, and friends.

Because of the force of your pains, what the bible says or whatever consolation is given to you becomes meaningless at that moment. You will be hit by a **CRISIS OF FAITH**! The things that matter to you will seem not to exist. Human solace will not bring comfort.

Only YOU and your openness to the Holy Spirit will help in overcoming the force of life's pains.

MEDITATION FOR THE DAY:

JESUS, I RECEIVE YOUR GRACE TO OVERCOME LIFE'S PAINS!

March 14:   Force of Pain (2)

That pain is unbearable is an understatement! It cuts through your heart and increases your blood pressure and if not careful, it can break your body (sickness, disease, and eventually - death). I learned a few things when the pain from my tragic loss was eating me up:

1. Find a point of contact to diffuse the destructive potential in your pain. For me, it was spiritual-soul-lifting music and service.

2. The greatest point of contact is acknowledging the sovereignty of God and His love for you, no matter how and what you feel about the pains. This one is hard to bear and comprehend!

As humans, we want to know "the why", and "the reason" we had to go through circumstances that bring such pain. We call to mind our good works, faithfulness, mistakes, and so on.

One fact is this – pain comes with our living on earth.

MEDITATION FOR THE DAY:

HOLY SPIRIT, BE MY POINT OF CONTACT IN LIFE'S CHALLENGES.

March 15: Pain Trapped

The pang of pain, like a subtle trap, will fizzle out the essence of living. One man - Job (in the bible) comes to mind, how he escaped the trap of pain after the loss of his children, businesses, properties, unsupportive spouse, and even his health:

1. Job expressed the hurt he felt and his suffering from pain. Do not lock yourself in, don't bottle up the emotions, pour them out to God, family, and friends.
2. He was open and frank with God about how he felt, but he never disregarded, nor disrespected God.

When the thick claw of pain digs deep into your soul, don't fall into the trap of isolation and resentment toward God or people.

If we get trapped, we deny ourselves access to God's healing and may end up with a life filled with bitterness and hate.

MEDITATION FOR THE DAY:

JESUS, I OPEN UP MY HEART TO YOUR ENDLESS GRACE IN TIMES OF PAIN.

March 16: Agony of Pain

I was a few minutes into the United States when the weight of the following week's outcome erupted in my heart. I was already a shadow of myself going through the pain of seeing the health deterioration of a loved one. Experiencing the pang of death was double jeopardy!

1. You may be going through a situation that seems to have no end (I know how this feels). Take great assurance in this life-changing statement in God's word: "THIS TOO SHALL PASS." How? I cannot explain fully in this short write-up, but you will eventually overcome the pain.

The memories will not leave you with ease, the anguish and discomforts will greet you intermittently as you journey through life. God's only son went through pain so that we will not go through the anguish of pain.

Whatever you are going through, let Jesus be your healing balm.

MEDITATION FOR THE DAY:

JESUS, HEAL MY HEART FROM LIFE'S PAINS.

March 17:   Pain-Free

Living our lives on earth free from the absence of pain is impossible. However, we can live a life of triumph over the effect and negative impact of pain. "But thanks [be] to God, who always leads us in triumph in the Christ... (2 Corinthians 2:14)". Few things from God's perspectives:

1. In this godless world you will continue to experience difficulties. But take heart! I have conquered the world (John 16:33 MSG). You are a conqueror!

2. He renews our hopes and heals our bodies (Psalms 147:3 CEV). Believe this!

Can we be free from pain? Yes! Do not forget, we are pilgrims on the earth. Life continues after death– when we will hunger, nor thirst anymore, and God will wipe every tear from our eyes (giving us eternal comfort) –Rev 7:16-17 AMP

MEDITATION FOR THE DAY:

IN CHRIST, I AM FREE FROM THE IMPACT OF PAIN!

March 18:   Every Other Thing

We live in a world of needs and wants. An environment where what we have or strive to own determines how people see and relate to us. But in God's economy which is bigger than the global economy, your needs and wants hinge on this:

1. Seek the Kingdom of God above all else, and live righteously, and he will give you everything you need (Matthew 6:33 NLT)

Seeking, for one thing, gives you access to every other thing. That one thing is to allow the attitude and character of God to shape our lives.

This is a major struggle for humanity to grasp, but also the greatest exposed secret to maximizing the richness of your life!

MEDITATION FOR THE DAY:

ALL THINGS ARE MINE IN JESUS' NAME!

March 19:   Him or Need

In our quest to have our needs met, we are confronted with the truth of what is most important to us – God or the need. God wants all our needs met, but His ultimate desire is for us to seek Him first, before our needs. God wants you to need Him first because:

1. The earth belongs to God! Everything in all the world is his! (Psalms 24:1 TLB)

2. You can be sure that God will take care of everything you need, his generosity exceeds even yours in the glory that pours from Jesus (Philippians 4:19 MSG)

The heightened demands for survival and achieving our dreams and goals have increased the temptation to seek God for our needs rather than seek Him above our needs (putting the cart before the horse).

Make a conscious decision today to seek HIM above your need – in Him consist of all that you will ever need in life.

MEDITATION FOR THE DAY:

IN CHRIST, ALL MY NEEDS ARE MET!

March 20: Be Worry-less

Being worried about our wants or needs is not inhuman, but allowing the emotions to lead us into anxiety, depression, and being overwhelmed is unproductive. How does God expect you to act in times of dire need?

1. Do not worry about anything; instead, pray about everything. Tell God what you need and thank him for all he has done (Philippians 4:6 NLT)
2. Let him have all your worries and cares, for he is always thinking about you and watching everything that concerns you (1 Peter 5:7 TLB)

God penned these thoughts because you and I can act upon them. God will never ask us to do what He knows we cannot do. You can WORRY-LESS.

You are like God - For we know that our life in this world is His life lived in us (1 John 4:17 NLV)

MEDITATION FOR THE DAY:

I LAY MY CARES AND BURDENS AT THE FEET OF JESUS.

March 21:   God Knows

The Omniscient (all-knowing) nature of God puts Him in a position where nothing in the universe happens without His knowledge. This great God knows YOU!

1. Therefore do not worry *or* be anxious (perpetually uneasy, distracted), saying, 'What are we going to eat?' or 'What are we going to drink?' or 'What are we going to wear?' (Matthew 6:31 AMP)
2. Pile your troubles on God's shoulders—he'll carry your load; he'll help you out (Psalms 55:22 MSG)

You were not created to be miserable! Accept God's invitation today:

"Are you weary, carrying a heavy burden? Then come to me. I will refresh your life, for I am your oasis. Simply join your life with mine. Learn my ways and you will discover that I am gentle, humble, and easy to please. (Matthew 11:28-29 TPT)

MEDITATION FOR THE DAY: THANK YOU, LORD, FOR BEARING MY CARE AND BURDENS.

March 22: Prayer for You

It is our day to pray. As you meditate on these prayer thoughts, this is God's promise for you: "Those who look to him for help will be radiant with joy; no shadow of shame will darken their faces (Psalms 34:5 - NLT)"

- Holy Spirit you are my point of contact through life's challenges.
- Jesus, I open my heart to your endless grace in times of pain and sorrow.
- Jesus, heal my heart from life's hurts, pains, and unpleasant circumstances.
- In Christ, I am free from the effect and impact of life's pains.
- All things are mine; I lack nothing!
- In Christ, all my needs are met!
- I lay all my cares and burdens at the feet of Jesus Christ.

MEDITATION FOR THE DAY:

THANK YOU, LORD, FOR BEARING MY CARES AND BURDENS.

March 23: Simplicity of Humility

The pursuit of relevance in life is one innate desire that drives most of us. How we reach our goals or meet our targets seem not to matter, until the sting of ignoring the simplicity of humility kicks in.

1. Many people reached their goals, but the lack of being humble made them crumble.
2. As simple as "Humility" sounds, its place in your life determines how far you make progress in strategic relationships.

The rise and fall of kings, presidents, and leaders in different spheres of life can be traced to how they acted with the attitude of humility. This is one virtue we all struggle with at some point in our life.

The earlier we master it, the wiser we become and avoid many pitfalls.

MEDITATION FOR THE DAY:

I WILL WALK IN THE SIMPLICITY OF HUMILITY DAILY.

March 24: Miracles in Humility

One of the mysteries of humility is the unlimited miracles it can produce in our lives if we embrace it. We have consciously and unconsciously closed doors of opportunities for the next level in our lives because:

1. We underestimated the looks, demeanor, challenges, and current state of what others are going through in their lives.
2. We present ourselves as one that knows it all, has it all and does not need the counsel or advice of others.

A more dangerous path is the arrogance with which we approach God. The Pharisee in the bible prayed: "God, I thank you that I am not greedy, dishonest, and unfaithful in marriage like other people" (Luke 18:11 CEV).

There are miracles locked up in being humble – do not let YOU and the world make you fumble!

MEDITATION FOR THE DAY:

I RESIST THE GRIP OF ARROGANCE IN MY LIFE IN JESUS' NAME!

March 25: Pride-O-Meter

I had the rare privilege to work with an energetic, brilliant, and dogged boss. During one of our moments together, he asked me: "Osebor, am I proud? Why do people say that I am proud?" Are you wondering how I responded to him?

1. At some point, you need to check your pride level. Note: "First pride, then the crash—the bigger the ego, the harder the fall (Proverbs 16:18 MSG)"
2. What you have achieved, whom you have become, and the things that are working out for you - are all under the control of God

"A man can receive nothing [he can claim nothing at all] unless it has been granted to him from heaven [for there is no other source than the sovereign will of God] – John 3:27 AMP.

Have you had a pride check lately? Pause, do it now!

MEDITATION FOR THE DAY:

HOLY SPIRIT, EXAMINE MY PRIDE LEVEL AND ALIGN ME TO YOUR WILL.

March 26: Humility in Divinity

An amazing reflection of the nature of humility is seen and manifested in the character of the Godhead – The Father, Son, and the Holy Spirit. It is worrisome that humans with some measure of power given to us, still struggle with being humble.

1. "Behold, God is mighty, and yet does not despise anyone [nor regard any as trivial] – Job 36:5 AMP
2. "Simply join your life with mine. Learn my ways and you will discover that I am gentle, humble, easy to please... – Matthew 11:29 TPT.

It is humbling to know that God – the Father of creation stoops low to relate with us in our human frailties. Walking in humility does not come with ease except by the Holy Spirit!

You can be humble – you are created in the image of the Godhead!

MEDITATION FOR THE DAY:

I WALK IN THE SPIRIT OF HUMILITY IN EVERY AREA OF MY LIFE.

March 27: Pride Creep

There are scopes of pride levels God can expect from us. Pride in who we are in Christ, the make-up of our being, or S.H.A.P.E (Spiritual gifts, Heart, Abilities, Personality, and Experiences). But God can never tolerate our pride and arrogance because of:

1. The things we have or possess. "...For a man's real life in no way depends upon the number of his possessions." (Luke 12:15 – PHILIPS)
2. Our sense of superiority, intelligence, position, or status over others. "So, beware if you think it could never happen to you, lest your pride becomes your downfall" (1 Corinthians 10:12 – TPT)

These are the dangerous paths that lead to 'PRIDE CREEP'! God still visits with the "Nebuchadnezzar experience": "King Nebuchadnezzar, this kingdom is no longer yours. You will be forced to live with the wild animals, away from people" (Daniel 4:30-33). This will not be your story – stay humble.

MEDITATION FOR THE DAY: LORD JESUS, I GIVE MY CROWNS AND TROPHIES TO YOU!

March 28: Pride Signpost (1)

It is extremely difficult for many of us to admit that we have some deep measure of pride in ourselves until we experience a sudden fall. For the next three series, we will be looking at the signs of pride in our lives. The signs of pride are:

1. Assuming you already know something when someone is teaching or talking.
2. Seeing yourself as too good to perform certain tasks.
3. Being too proud to ask for help.
4. Thinking you are better than others who are different or less fortunate.

Take a good look at the list above. Some of these signs can creep into your life without you being aware of their existence.

We will look at more of this tomorrow.

MEDITATION FOR THE DAY:

SEARCH MY HEART O GOD, MAKE ME MORE LIKE YOU.

March 29: Pride Signpost (2)

Your pride signpost can mess you up when you least expect it. It is imperative that you and I fight with everything that is in us, to resist our human tendencies to be proud. See more signs:

1. Talking about Yourself a lot
2. When You disregard the advice of others
3. When You are Consistently Critical
4. The consistent need for attention and affirmation
5. Overly obsessed with your physical appearance

Pride cripples the unimaginable promises God has in stock for you. The inventory of God's blessings for you is exceedingly, abundantly, and far above all that you can ever think. Do not let pride cripple your amazing life!

We will wrap this up tomorrow.

MEDITATION FOR THE DAY:

LORD JESUS, RE-MOULD MY LIFE TO LIVE FOR YOU ALONE!

March 30: Arrogantly Proud

Some individuals are 'proudly proud' – those who take pride as a way of life, not minding whose feeling is hurt because of their actions. Are you:

1. Unable to receive constructive criticism?
2. Unwilling to submit to authority?
3. Ignoring people's attempts to communicate with you?
4. Justifying your Sin instead of admitting it?
5. Name-dropping: Pretending to be who you are not so that you can be accepted into another social class.

The story of the Ostrich in the Bible (Job 39:13-18) is an eye-opener. Pride can make you consciously neglect the important things and deprive you of God's wisdom and understanding in mastering the issues of life.

Take a break today and cultivate the virtue of humility before it becomes too late for regrets.

MEDITATION FOR THE DAY:

HOLY SPIRIT, TEACH ME TO BE HUMBLE & SUBMISSIVE TO YOU.

March 31: Pride-Spot

Pride creates a subtle blind spot many of us are not aware of. I once worked with an intelligent employer whose pride spot caused the closure of a promising multi-billion-dollar company. Anytime we begin to exhibit an attitude of superiority over others:

1. We are unconsciously creating pride-spots that will be detrimental to our downfall.

2. We create a relationship vacuum that could have filled up the pride spots we created.

Your pride-spots are those places in your life that open avenues for failures, rejection, and isolation. We all know these spots.

I pray we'll do the needful to avoid Pride-Spots in our lives

MEDITATION FOR THE DAY:

HOLY SPIRIT, I YIELD COMPLETELY TO YOU. HELP ME OVERCOME MY PRIDE SPOTS.

April 1: Prayer for You

Welcome to the month of April and the beginning of the second quarter of the year. I believe in God and receive on your behalf the fulfillment of His promises for you in this new quarter in Jesus' name! Please make these bold declarations:

- I will walk in the simplicity of humility daily.
- I resist the grip of arrogance in my life in Jesus' name.
- I walk in the spirit of humility in every area of my life.
- Jesus, I lay my crowns and trophies at your feet.
- Search my heart o God, make me more like you.
- Jesus, remold my life to live for you alone.
- Holy Spirit, teach me to be humble and submissive to you.
- I am God's exclusively – I walk daily in the spirit of humility!

MEDITATION FOR THE DAY:

ALL MY EXPECTATIONS SHALL COME TO FRUITION, IN JESUS' NAME!

April 2: Expectations

The word expectation means a strong belief that something will happen or be the case in the future. The ugly circumstances of life have taken a toll on many of us, and we seem to have given up on expecting that the best is yet to come.

1. God wants you to see the brighter side of life no matter what you have gone through or going through and will go through.
2. It is almost impossible to have or receive what you do not expect (belief will happen to or for you).

The human mind can easily expect negative things to happen more than good things.

But Job in the Bible, during his intense suffering said: "All the days of my hard service I will wait, till my change comes." (Job 14:14 NKJV)

MEDITATION FOR THE DAY:

FATHER, I WILL WAIT ON YOU, UNTIL MY CHANGE COMES!

April 3: Ask, Seek, and Knock

No doubt, we all expect good, better, and greater things to happen to us in life. However, your expectations are hinged on the principles of "ASKING, SEEKING, AND KNOCKING" and not complaining or worrying. Expectations say:

1. For everyone who keeps on asking receives.
2. He or she who keeps on seeking finds.
3. And to him or her who keeps on knocking it will be opened.

These principles work when we expect in faith. "But he or she must ask in faith, without doubting (God's willingness to help) …" James 1:6 – AMP.

What are you expecting? keep asking, seeking, and knocking in faith with thanksgiving.

MEDITATION FOR THE DAY:

THANK YOU, JESUS, FOR BRINGING MY EXPECTATIONS TO PASS!

April 4: Be Expectant

God is concerned about seeing your expectations met. Read His position about bringing your expectations to pass in (Matthew 7:9-11 - AMP):

1. "Or what man/woman is there among you who, if his son/daughter asks for bread, will (instead) give him/her a stone?

2. "Or if he/she asks for a fish, will (instead) give him/her a snake?

3. "If you then, evil (sinful by nature) as you are, know how to give good and advantageous gifts to your children, how much more will your Father who is in heaven (perfect as He is) give what is good and advantageous to those who keep asking Him.

God – our Father is willing to go the extra mile (this he has proven by the death of His precious son Jesus) to see your expectations come to pass.

Rejoice, because your expectations will not be cut short!

MEDITATION FOR THE DAY: THANK YOU, JESUS, FOR BRINGING MY EXPECTATIONS TO PASS!

April 5: A Good Father

Our experiences with our biological fathers affect our perception of God and our trust that He will bring to pass our expectations. Never compare God with human parents no matter what you are going through, because:

1. He has by his own action given us everything that is necessary for living the truly good life (2 Peter 1:3 JB Philips)

2. Every good thing is given, and every perfect gift is from above; it comes down from the Father of lights [the Creator and Sustainer of the heavens] – (James 1:17 AMP)

The creator and sustainer of your life – God, is a GOOD FATHER! He wants to give you more than just good things. He loves you so much and has promised not to withhold anything good from you.

Waste no time, commune with Him today!

MEDITATION FOR THE DAY:

LORD, YOU'RE A GOOD FATHER, I'M LOVED BY YOU.

April 6: Promise Keeper

As a teenager, we had a name for 'uncles and aunties' who would not keep their promises after running errands for them – "uncle/aunty promise and fail". I announce to you today, that you have a God, a Father, who is a PROMISE KEEPER.

1. God's promises are His words, and His words are His bond. "That's how it is with my words. They don't return to me without doing everything I send them to do." (Isaiah 55:11 CEV)

2. "Not one of the good promises which the Lord had spoken to the house of Israel failed; all had come to pass" (Joshua 21:45 AMP). Yours will!

What has God promised you in the closet? "And because of his glory and excellence, he has given us great and precious promises (2 Peter 1:4 NLT)".

Get excited! Your expectations will come to pass.

MEDITATION FOR THE DAY:

MY FATHER, YOU'RE FAITHFUL TO KEEP YOUR PROMISES TO ME!

April 7: An Expected End

Every journey or endeavor has the promise of an expected outcome. However, because we may not fully comprehend what happens in the process of time, we struggle with doubts, fears, and unbelief before our expectations come to fruition.

1. For I know the thoughts that I think toward you, saith the Lord, thoughts of peace, and not of evil, to give you an expected end" (Jeremiah 29:11 KJV)

For all you will ever go through, God has seen the end. "From the very beginning, I told what would happen long before it took place". (Isaiah 46:10 CEV).

For your peace of mind, trust God's thoughts toward you!

MEDITATION FOR THE DAY:

ALL THAT IS GOOD FOR ME, GOD WILL SURELY BRING TO PASS!

April 8: Expecting with Joy

The state of your heart is key during the period of waiting for an expected end. Negative emotions such as anger, bitterness, fears, doubts, unbelief, and negative confessions will rob you of the joy of expectations. You must come to terms that:

1. Every expectation you are looking forward to has been scheduled in God's calendar.
2. What you do or how you feel will not alter the schedule. We need caution not to extend it with our actions.

"God makes everything happen at the right time. Yet none of us can ever fully understand all he has done, and he puts questions in our minds about the past and the future" (Ecclesiastes 3:11 CEV).

Make it a responsibility to expect joy today.

MEDITATION FOR THE DAY:

THANK YOU, JESUS. MY EXPECTATIONS ARE MET!

April 9: Believing vs Expecting

The word "believing" has become our modest way of affirming faith in God, but within us lies flickers of doubt. What guarantees the outcome of your expectations?

1. Hear from God. What did God say to you about the things you are expecting? What did He say about them in the Bible?
2. Do what He says. God honors His words when we act on them! Some instructions come from hearing from God – please do them!

God will meet and surpass your expectations. "He will achieve infinitely more than your greatest request, your most unbelievable dream, and exceed your wildest imagination! He will outdo them all, for his miraculous power constantly energizes you" (Ephesians 3:20 TPT).

Instead of saying I am believing God; rather declare 'I AM EXPECTING GREAT THINGS FROM GOD'!

MEDITATION FOR THE DAY:

THANK YOU, LORD, FOR EXCEEDING MY EXPECTATIONS!

April 10: He Will Do It

The third guarantee that your expectations will come to pass is, God will do it!

1. "Remember what happened long ago. Remember that I am God, and there is no other God. I am God, and there is no one like me... I will make what I have said come true; I will do what I have planned." (Isaiah 46:8 and 11 NCV)

2. He who calls you will do it because he is faithful. (1 Thessalonians 5:24 GNT)

The irony of our relationship with God is that we expect Him to meet our needs, but we don't feel God has needs He expects us to meet too – obeying Him, serving Jesus, serving others, and walking with the Holy Spirit.

The greatest secret to having ALL that you expect is this: "and he will give them to you if you give him first place in your life and live as he wants you to" (Matthew 6:33 TLB). It is on God's terms!

MEDITATION FOR THE DAY:

LORD JESUS, I GIVE YOU THE FIRST PLACE IN MY LIFE!

April 11: Prayer for You

The peace of mind we need as we expect great things is God's revelation – "'Call to me and I will answer you. I'll tell you marvelous and wondrous things that you could never figure out on your own.' (Jeremiah 33:3 MSG)

- Father, I will wait on you, until my change comes.
- Thank you, Jesus, for bringing my expectations to reality.
- Heavenly Father, you are a good Father, and I am loved by you.
- My Father, you are faithful to keep your promises to me.
- All that is good for me, God will surely bring to pass!
- Thank you, Lord, my expectations are met!
- Thank you, Father, for exceeding my expectations.

MEDITATION FOR THE DAY:

LORD JESUS, I RECEIVE GRACE TO CONTINUALLY GIVE YOU THE FIRST PLACE IN MY LIFE.

April 12: Life and Battles

Life is an array of battles that cuts across every sphere of our human existence. The battle for life, health, relationships, wealth, dreams, and fulfillment is unending. Some we survive, some break us, while some drain us. The reality is this:

1. We live in a world under the control of an adversary who exists for our downfall. But God has sovereignty.
2. Everything you will ever have or have had will be through a fight!

Sometimes, I wonder why we go through these battles in life. Why can't we live a peaceful and stressless life on earth? The answer: "it will be terrible for the earth and the sea because the devil has come down to you! He is filled with anger (Revelation 12:12 NCV)".

Life is warfare you have been designed to overcome!

MEDITATION FOR THE DAY:

I AM DESTINED TO OVERCOME LIFE'S BATTLES!

April 13: The Enemy's Target

The best of creation is you! You are created in the likeness of the Godhead, and you command the love and attention of heaven. This reality of yours angers the devil so much, that his lifetime missions' statement is to:

1. Steal your glory, joy, position, and blessings.
2. Kill your dreams and eventually your physical existence.
3. Destroy everything that makes living on earth worthwhile for you.

In any battle, there is always a key target. You and I are the enemy's target. Everything the devil does is targeted to harm and cause us pain. But "thanks be to God, who always gives us the victory in Christ" (2 Corinthians 2:14 NMB).

You have no reason to be overwhelmed with life's battles; greater is He that is in you!

MEDITATION FOR THE DAY:

I AM THE APPLE OF GOD'S EYE; I AM AN OVERCOMER!

April 14: Understanding the Enemy

The enemy has one agenda – to cause you sorrow or annihilate you from the face of the earth. Do you know who the enemy is? Do you think it's a family member? A close ally?

1. For we are not fighting against people made of flesh and blood, but against persons without bodies—the evil rulers of the unseen world,

2. those mighty satanic beings and great evil princes of darkness who rule this world, and against huge numbers of wicked spirits in the spirit world.

The enemy manipulates and uses people to accomplish his agenda; people who are consciously or unconsciously contending with the fulfillment of God's promises in your life.

Rejoice at what God – Your Father says: "Whoever attacks you, does it without my consent; whoever fights against you will fall" (Isaiah 54:15 GNT).

MEDITATION FOR THE DAY: I HAVE THE VICTORY OVER PRINCIPALITIES AND POWERS IN THE NAME OF JESUS!

April 15: Battle-Proof (1)

It is an age-long history that the battle of life is more spiritual than physical. How do we successfully fight against unforeseen forces? God in His infinite knowledge has shared with us in Ephesians 6:14-17 Amplified version:

1.   Live a life of truth (personal integrity and moral courage).
2.   Have an upright heart.
3.   Be a person who seeks peace as best as you can.

The enemy uses lies, deception, and stirring of strife as some of his/her strategies to rule over our lives. But the Bible has given us eternal battle-winning secrets to counter the offense of the enemy. Choose God's wisdom on how to win unforeseen forces using people.

We will continue tomorrow on some of God's winning strategies.

MEDITATION FOR THE DAY:

I AM NOT IGNORANT OF THE ENEMY'S SCHEMES; I AM A VICTOR!

April 16: Battle-Proof (2)

God uses seemingly weak things to confound mighty things. His battle-winning plans look so easy to enforce, but many of us take them for granted. God says:

1. Lift the protective shield of Faith to extinguish all the flaming arrows of the evil one.
2. Accept and walk in the salvation God has given to you in Christ Jesus.
3. Use the sword of the spirit – the word of God to fight against the unseen forces.
4. Engage in prayers – praying in the spirit for others, yourself, and your purpose.

Every battle-proof strategy God gave to us in the Bible still works! The devil tried Jesus with several temptations, He overcame the devil using these strategies – and with the help of the Holy Spirit.

You too can overcome it with the help of the Holy Spirit.

MEDITATION FOR THE DAY:

I AM BATTLE-PROOFED BY THE HOLY SPIRIT TO OVERCOME LIFE CHALLENGES!

April 17: Your Mind Warfare

No doubt the battles of life, whether spiritual or physical, are lost and won in the mind. The happenings in our environment set our mind on battles, however:

1. Every child of God defeats this evil world.
2. We achieve this victory through our faith.

"We do live in the world, but we do not fight in the same way the world fights. We fight with weapons that are different from those the world uses. Our weapons have power from God that can destroy the enemy's strong places (2 Corinthians 10:3-5)". Are you a child of God? Do you accept Jesus as your Lord? Do you believe in what the Bible says?

Your response is your victory access to winning mind-warfare.

MEDITATION FOR THE DAY:

I AM A CHILD OF GOD, I OVERCOME THE BATTLES OF LIFE IN JESUS NAME!

April 18: Potent Weapon

After his fall, Lucifer became an accuser of you and me, bringing charges of our sinful behaviors before God, day and night (Revelation 12:7-11). The earth became the seat of his evil atrocities. Two potent weapons God has given us to defeat the devil:

1. The blood of the lamb.
2. The word of your testimony.

The shed blood of Jesus remains the greatest battle weapon for you and me. Jesus' death is God's sacrifice used to liberate us from the power of sin, death, sickness, and life's struggles.

As you acknowledge this, declare, and share it with others, your victory over life's battles is guaranteed.

MEDITATION FOR THE DAY:

I OVERCOME BY THE BLOOD OF JESUS AND THE WORD OF MY TESTIMONIES!

April 19: Bloody Friday

A common sight in war zones in addition to lifeless bodies and chopped human limbs is BLOOD! Wars are bloody, and so also the battles we go through (though invisible). Over 2000years ago, on a Friday, the blood of a sinless man was shed:

1. But he was wounded for the wrong we did; he was crushed for the evil we did.
2. The punishment, which made us well, was given to him, and we are healed because of his wounds. (Isaiah 53:5 – NCV)

This bloody Friday has made available to us, the most potent weapon to overcome sin, sickness, poverty, evil attacks, failures, disappointment, and even death!

As we remember the story of Christ's death on the cross, be thankful that your victory in life was sealed and delivered too!

MEDITATION FOR THE DAY:

IN ALL THINGS, I AM MORE THAN A CONQUEROR THROUGH THE BLOOD OF JESUS!

April 20: Hopeless Battle

I have been through some intense personal battles, and I got to a point where I felt all hope was lost. I was faithless, stranded, and felt defeated. This verse from the song 'God moves in a mysterious way" renewed my strength:

> "Ye fearful saints, fresh courage take
> The clouds you so much dread
> Are big with mercy and shall break
> In blessings on your head".

Do you feel drained and worn out from the battles that seem endless? The death of Jesus, after the crucifixion, was like a hopeless battle for believers. At night we may cry, but when morning comes, we will celebrate!

Fix your gaze on Jesus, you have overcome the battles.

MEDITATION FOR THE DAY:

I KNOW MY REDEEMER LIVES; I AM BORN TO REIGN IN LIFE!

April 21: Strife Over

The most devastating moments in life are when we have done all we can and made every effort to succeed, but all seem to be in vain. That is not your case as a child of God. Your victory is already assured at the cross and resurrection of Jesus Christ:

> The strife is o'er, the battle done;
> The victory of life is won;
> The song of triumph has begun:
> Alleluia!

The resurrection of Jesus Christ silenced every effect of strife, struggles, and battles you will ever encounter in life! Never live your life being hopeless or feeling perpetually discouraged.

Christ is risen to die no more but to give you victory always.

MEDITATION FOR THE DAY:

MY BATTLES ARE OVER; MY VICTORY IS GUARANTEED IN THE NAME OF JESUS!

April 22: Prayer for You

The resurrection of Jesus Christ gave you victory over sickness, poverty, and death! It gave you unlimited access: "If you remain in me and follow my teachings, you can ask anything you want, and it will be given to you." (John 15:7 NCV)

- I am destined to overcome life's battles!
- I have the victory over principalities and powers in the name of Jesus!
- I am not ignorant of the enemy's schemes; I am a victor!
- I am battle-proofed by the Holy Spirit to overcome life's challenges!
- I overcome by the blood of Jesus and the word of my testimonies!
- In all things, I am more than a conqueror through the blood of Jesus!
- My battles are over; my victory is guaranteed in the name of Jesus!

MEDITATION FOR THE DAY:

I HAVE COMPLETE VICTORY IN EVERY AREA OF YOUR LIFE! IT IS IN JESUS CHRIST!

April 23: What you Say

Every passing day is filled with statements, comments, and thoughts that govern the outcomes of our work, business, career, relationships, and eventually our self-worth in life. There is a unique dimension to what we say from God's word:

1. The universe was created and beautifully coordinated by the power of God's words.
2. He spoke and the invisible realm gave birth to all that is seen. (Hebrews 11:3 TPT)

The words you say have creative power – whether positive or negative. The world has been designed to respond or react to what you say. Your life was created by words, and it will be sustained by what you say.

What do you say daily?

MEDITATION FOR THE DAY:

MY WORLD IS FRAMED BY THE WORDS OF GOD!

April 24: Word Content

The 2nd Edition of the 20-volume Oxford English Dictionary contains full entries for 171,476 words in current use, and 47,156 obsolete words (google search). We have access to a great number of words to build or destroy our lives and others.

1. The words you speak are not ordinary. They are seeds that have good and bad fruits in them. It works like the Law of sowing and reaping.
2. What you say carries life – they become your reality. Watch your words!

The contents of your words mirror who you are. What you spend your time on – watching, listening, or reading is forming your word content. Word-contents are raw materials for creation.

Let God's words be your content; become LIMITLESS!

MEDITATION FOR THE DAY:

MY WORDS CARRY LIFE; I WILL BE MINDFUL OF WHAT I SAY!

April 25: Power in Words

The creation of the human spirit, soul, and body is one of the mysteries of life. We tend to allow the cravings of our body and the longings of our soul to relegate the power of what we say. You are a spirit being and so are your words, they:

1. Have the power of life and death in them – your words can make or destroy you and others.
2. Are controlled by the force of the spirit that controls your life.

We are spirit beings dwelling in a body with a soul. You were not designed to be controlled by your body or soul – but by your spirit.

Hence, if your spirit is controlled by the devil, you will speak evil and foul words, but if controlled by God, you will speak good!

MEDITATION FOR THE DAY:

MY WORDS ARE GOD-CONTROLLED!

April 26: Bridle Your Tongue

We live in a generation that believes strongly in: "speaking out your mind', 'claiming your rights', 'being insensitive to the emotions of others', and so on. Unfortunately, your tongue and your mouth are the channels to unleash these human tendencies:

1. The tongue is not able to be tamed. It is a fickle, unrestrained evil that spews out words full of toxic poison.
2. We use our tongues to praise God our Father and then turn around and curse a person who was made in his very image.

The mastery of life starts with the mastery of what we say. The temptation to react sharply or brashly to others is high when we are angry. Your true personality is revealed under pressure and what you say at those moments matters!

Train your mouth to trap your tongue – YOUR WORDS MATTER!

MEDITATION FOR THE DAY:

I RECEIVE MASTERY OVER THE WORDS OF MY MOUTH IN JESUS' NAME!

April 27: Word Control

The heart, the tongue, and the mouth are strategic parts of our body that are influenced to release gracious or destructive words from within us. However, you can control what you say:

1. Do not let any part of your body become an instrument of evil to serve sin. Instead, give yourselves completely to God.
2. Use your whole body as an instrument to do what is right for the glory of God.

As humans, we often falter in the things we say. God wants our whole body controlled by His words - including your tongue and mouth. People who think they are religious but say things they should not say are just fooling themselves. Their "religion" is worth nothing (James 1:26 NCV).

Get control of your words today!

MEDITATION FOR THE DAY:

I HAVE CONTROL OVER WHAT I SAY BY THE POWER OF THE HOLY SPIRIT!

April 28: Deflect Anger

Mastering the art of relationship with God and people is one amazing secret to gaining speed in life. But many of us have lost countless opportunities, strained valuable relationships, and closed doors because of our poor choice of words.

1. A gentle answer deflects anger, but harsh words make tempers flare
2. The tongue of the wise makes knowledge appealing, but the mouth of a fool belches out foolishness.

We can be constructive with our words – uplifting and strengthening others, seeing the best of them. "Be gracious in your speech. The goal is to bring out the best in others in a conversation, not to put them down, not cut them out (Colossians 4:6 MSG)".

You can deflect anger through the gentleness of your response.

MEDITATION FOR THE DAY:

MY WORDS SHALL BE GRACIOUS AND SOUL-LIFTING!

April 29: Kill or Give Life

Dear friends, do not take your words lightly! Our physical world was formed by words! Your words form your life, your relationships, your business, your career, your family, and your finances. Why take what you say for granted? Proverbs 18:21:

1. Words kill, words give life; they are either poison or fruit—you choose (MSG).
2. Those who love to talk will suffer the consequences. Men have died for saying the wrong thing! (TLB)
3. Your words are so powerful that they will kill or give life, and the talkative person will reap the consequences (TPT).
4. Words can bring death or life! Talk too much, and you will eat everything you say (CEV).

Do I still need to list more?

Choose to speak the right words every day!

MEDITATION FOR THE DAY:

I CHOOSE TO SPEAK WORDS THAT GIVE LIFE TO ME AND OTHERS!

April 30: Your Heart Speaks

The core of every human being is his or her heart. The heart holds and retains the raw materials used to construct your words and eventually your WORLD! Your heart is so key because your desires, passions, prayers, and future, rise from there.

1. "For whatever is in your heart determines what you say (Matthew 12:34 NLT)"
2. As a face is reflected in water, so the heart reflects the real person (Proverbs 27:19 NLT)

A great quote that has given me guidance in my heart management is: "whatever enters your heart, has entered your life".

I watch what enters my life. "Guard your heart above all else, for it determines the course of your life (Proverbs 4:23 NLT)."

MEDITATION FOR THE DAY:

I GUARD MY HEART WITH THE WORDS OF GOD ONLY!

May 1: Think about what you say

Your thought process fuels the release of what you say. The world is controlled by words and words give meaning to the things that exist in your life and environment. You were designed to say things that represent your god-nature. Summing it all up, friends, I would say you will do best by:

1. Filling your minds and meditating on things true, noble, reputable, authentic, compelling, gracious—the best, not the worst; the beautiful, not the ugly; things to praise, not things to curse. Philippians 4:8 MSG

Who you are today is truly by the grace of God, the reality of your thoughts and "sayings". Do you want to see a better and greater version of yourself tomorrow?

Think before you say who that person or others should be...

HAPPY NEW MONTH!

MEDITATION FOR THE DAY:

MY THOUGHTS AND WORDS ARE SEASONED WITH WHAT GOD SAYS!

May 2: Prayer for You

We try daily to be the best we can be in every area of our lives. My prayer for you is: "Let the kindness of the Lord our God be with us. Make us successful in everything we do. Yes, make us successful in everything we do (Psalms 90:17 GW)"

- My world is framed by the words of God!
- My words carry life; I am mindful of the things I say!
- My words are God-controlled!
- I receive mastery over the words of my mouth in the name of Jesus!
- I have control over what I say by the power of the Holy Spirit!
- My words shall be gracious and soul-lifting!
- I choose to speak words that give life to me and others!
- My heart is guarded by the words of God only!

MEDITATION FOR THE DAY:

MY THOUGHTS AND WORDS ARE SEASONED WITH GOD'S!

May 3: Time to Manifest

Our world is going through so much turmoil and it is increasingly difficult to get a grip on it. We hear news daily that breaks our hearts – sudden deaths, troubles everywhere, strange happenings, and so on. But wait a minute:

1. You have been created to live in this era to bring solutions to these issues.
2. The entire universe is standing on tiptoe, yearning to see the unveiling of God's glorious sons and daughters! (Romans 8:19 TPT)

The problem in our world is unending. The suffering and challenges of many will be on the increase. However, God is counting on you and me to step into the situation to reveal His love, glory, and power to mankind.

Your manifestation in life is tied to your willingness to partner with God to solve problems for others.

MEDITATION FOR THE DAY:

MY TIME TO MANIFEST IS NOW!

May 4: Think About Others

The intense demands to meet personal needs and achieve goals that serve 'me, myself, and I" have taken many of us off the path of relevance and announcement to the world. Your relevance in life is tied to:

1. The victories you attained during and over your struggles and challenges despite all odds.
2. The many individuals that found meaning and purpose because of your influence in their lives.

We live in a millennial-driven generation where all we think about is "ME", what happens to others is their business. God never intended that we live that way.

Your progress and fulfillment in life are to become more like God – who thinks about you every day and longs that you THINK ABOUT OTHERS too!

MEDITATION FOR THE DAY:

MY GOD, RID ME OF SELFISHNESS AND HELP ME TO BE SELFLESS IN JESUS' NAME!

May 5: Find Meaning

I am persuaded that everyone alive today is for a purpose – whether we agree or not is another subject of discussion. For me, life will be boring if there is no meaning in it – I find great meaning in seeing others moving forward in their lives as I make progress in mine.

1. Can you find meaning in your life? Do you find meaning or see purpose in the scheme of all that is happening around you?
2. What does being alive mean to you? Is it for self-purpose? God-purpose?

We can never find true meaning in life if it's just about us. Life is living the way God designed it – to "Prosper! Reproduce! Fill the Earth! Take charge! (Genesis 1:28 MSG)".

You are not alive to waste time on earth, you are living for a purpose – to give meaning to your life and others – FIND IT!

MEDITATION FOR THE DAY:

JESUS, HELP ME TO FIND MEANING DAILY IN LIFE.

May 6: Death to Self

It is increasingly difficult to find men and women who are willing to give their best to God and others. Many of us are living below our potential because we will rather pay more attention to our pursuits and neglect what matters most to God and His purposes. Jesus showed us the beauty of death-to-self:

1. "I must fall and die like a kernel of wheat that falls into the furrows of the earth. Unless I die I will be alone—a single seed. But my death will produce many new wheat kernels—a plentiful harvest of new lives" – John 12:24 TLB

God is not asking us to die literally for His benefit or others – He is asking you and me to break the culture of self-centeredness. Until you give your best – time, resources, talents, and gifts to the services of God and others, your life's potential will be limited. Life was designed for giving more than receiving.

MEDITATION FOR THE DAY:

JESUS, I YIELD MY BEST TO BRING YOU GLORY AND JOY TO OTHERS!

May 7: Release Yourself

At some point in life, we are opportune to visit the graveyard. We see tombs of people who fulfilled their dreams and many that were short-lived. Dreams are not fulfilled when you refuse to release yourself:

1. One person gives freely yet gains even more; another withholds unduly but comes to poverty (Proverbs 11:24 NIV)

2. Give these things without charging, since you received them without paying (Matthew 10:8 GW)

There are gifts, ideas, talents, skills, and experiences that are in you. You cannot allow the challenges of life to cripple what you can offer the world. Steve Jobs, the late CEO of Apple said, "Being the richest man in the cemetery doesn't matter to me ... Going to bed at night saying we've done something wonderful... that's what matters to me."

What matters to you comes to reality when you release yourself!

MEDITATION FOR THE DAY: JESUS, I'M ALL YOURS!

May 8: Break the Limits

Created within us is a deep longing to be more. But the issues of life and the glaring missing piece in our lives, have taken a strong toll on us, limiting our potential and capacity to be more. Be encouraged in this that:

1. No test or temptation that comes your way is beyond the course of what others have had to face.

2. All you need to remember is that God will never let you down; he will never let you be pushed past your limit; he'll always be there to help you come through it. (1 Corinthians 10:13 – MSG)

Life has thrown at me countless circumstances that broke me beyond what human ability could handle. God's word was my turning point – it brought healing and beautiful relationships that helped me to break limits.

You too can, God lives in YOU!

MEDITATION FOR THE DAY:

I CAN NOT BE LIMITED; GOD LIVES IN ME!

May 9: Maximize You

A close confidante, Pastor, and mentor's email signature have this quote: "I was born mud; I am determined to die marble... so help me God". Reading this each time I get an email from him re-enforces my passion to be the best I should be in life.

1. Living inside of you is God's Spirit that created the world – the one that is at work in you to maximize your potential.
2. For as you know him better, he will give you, through his great power, everything you need for living a truly good life (2 Peter 1:3 TLB)

Living a life below your capacity does not please God. It will never please you, that I know very well. You cannot go through life feeling knocked out and hopeless.

Brace yourself up, spread out your wings; maximize all that has been deposited in you!

MEDITATION FOR THE DAY:

I HAVE GOD'S ABILITY IN ME TO BE WHO HE CREATED ME TO BE!

May 10: Unlock Your Potentials

The world can be seen from different perspectives based on the lenses through which you look at it. Many people see problems, chaos, disasters, diseases, hunger, and lack, while others see opportunities, solutions, ideas, and gaps to fill.

1. What you see reveals the depth of your growth, maturity, and learning.
2. What you do after you see, depends on how you unlock and deploy your potential to react or respond to what you see.

Deep inside of you lie the solutions to your needs and the needs of others. Many of us are complacent about our challenges and less concerned about others.

Rise up today and unlock your potential – you have what it takes to make a mark in life!

MEDITATION FOR THE DAY:

I MUST RELEASE MY GOD-GIVEN ABILITIES TO SOLVE PROBLEMS IN MY ENVIRONMENT!

May 11: Fight for It

The battles against the fulfillment of your dreams, aspirations, and purpose can be overwhelming. The struggles of financial constraints, human disappointments, health challenges, delayed expectations, and many other issues can knock you out!

1. Life is a battleground that presents two options: WIN OR LOSE!

2. How can anyone break into a strong man's house and steal his things, unless he first ties up the strong man? Then he can take everything (Matthew 12:29 CEV)

Your joy, successes, and potential are under attack every day. The greatest mission of the enemy is to steal, kill and destroy the things that matter most to you – especially the ability to influence your world.

Do not take life for granted, fight for your place, for God has given you victory in Christ Jesus!

MEDITATION FOR THE DAY:

I HAVE THE VICTORY IN CHRIST JESUS!

May 12: Prayer for You

On this day, I ask that: 'God will cause you to shine forth like the brightness of the sun and turn your stress into STRENGTHS! Make these declarations:

- It is my season of manifestation in the name of Jesus!
- Jesus, rid me of selfishness, make me self-less!
- My God, help me to find meaning in life in Jesus' name!
- Jesus, I give myself away, so you can use me.
- I cannot be limited; God dwells in me!
- I release my God-given abilities to solve problems for myself and others!

MEDITATION FOR THE DAY:

I HAVE THE VICTORY OVER LIFE'S CHALLENGES IN JESUS' NAME!

May 13: Your Human Spirit

Human anatomy is majorly composed of three parts – the spirit, soul, and body. These three parts work as a team to make living on earth possible. Your human spirit can function in two realms – the physical and spiritual world. Thus:

1. Giving attention to its effective operation if you are still living on earth determines your progress.

2. The neglect of the growth of your human spirit is evident in most of the failures, disappointments, distractions, and confusions that are experienced in life.

Life can be difficult when our spirit is insensitive to the forces that control our world. We walk in the flesh, but our struggles and battles are more spiritual. The strength of your spirit determines your victories.

How do you grow spiritually? Let's unpack the answer to this question, tomorrow.

MEDITATION FOR THE DAY:

HOLY SPIRIT, TEACH ME TO STRENGTHEN MY HUMAN SPIRIT.

May 14: This Born-Again Mystery

How do we grow spiritually? How can the human spirit be empowered to function at its highest peak? The answer is not far-reaching, but it has become the hardest decision for many to accept for thousands of years:

1. Jesus answered, "Nicodemus, listen to this eternal truth: Before a person can perceive God's kingdom realm, they must first experience a rebirth." (John 3:3 TPT)

The new birth gives us access to the supernatural. Death and destruction await all humans daily, "but unless you repent [change your old way of thinking, turn from your sinful ways and live changed lives], you will likewise perish (Luke 13:5 AMP).

Growing spiritually starts with accepting Jesus Christ as your Lord and your Savior. Are you born again?

MEDITATION FOR THE DAY:

LORD JESUS, I REPENT OF MY SINS; I ACCEPT YOU AS MY LORD AND MY SAVIOR!

May 15: Thirsty and Hungry

How do we grow spiritually? What do you do when you are thirsty? How do you resolve the pang of hunger when it hits your stomach? As we do not trade anything to quench our thirst and hunger, so you cannot starve your human spirit.

1. In the same way that nursing infants cry for milk, you must intensely crave the pure spiritual milk of God's Word. For this "milk" will cause you to grow into maturity, fully nourished and strong for life (1 Peter 2:2 TPT)

Our physical body depends on food and drinks to grow, so your human spirit hunger and thirst for the word of God to grow. You are a spirit being that needs spiritual meat and milk to Grow.

Do not take the risk of ignoring a dose of God's word daily!

MEDITATION FOR THE DAY:

MY FATHER, I WILL SEEK YOUR WORD DAILY, FOR THE REJOICING OF MY LIFE.

May 16: Exchange through Meditation

How do we grow spiritually? Another way we grow spiritually is by developing our human spirit through meditation. Meditating on God's perspectives (the Bible) gives us an unusual dimension to the things human understanding cannot comprehend.

1. Meditation birth insights, inspirations, and divine understanding into your most challenging issues.
2. Meditation connects your human spirit to God's, and through this process exchange your weaknesses for the ability of God to confront earthly matters.

Negative thoughts, complaining, or worrying will not change any situation.

"Never stop reading The Book of the Law, day and night you must think about what it says. If you obey it completely, you will be able to take this land" (Joshua 1:8 CEV).

MEDITATION FOR THE DAY: I WILL THINK DAILY ABOUT GOD'S WORD, AND MY PATHS SHALL BE PROSPEROUS IN JESUS' NAME!

May 17: Confession Brings Possession

How do we grow spiritually? We become mature in the affairs of life and the things of the Spirit, as our words align with our mediation and the word of God. What you say, says a lot about you and registers in the spirit world.

1. The spirit world activates what you say in the natural world. You will always get what you say... Good or bad.

2. "With your whole being you embrace God setting things right, and then you say it, right out loud" (Romans 10:9 MSG)

The world was framed by God's confessions! When you boldly say what God says, then you possess the things you desire. Your confession gives you possessions.

Take sides with the words of God; your confessions will become your reality!

MEDITATION FOR THE DAY:

I SPEAK FAITH-FILLED WORDS THAT TRANSFORM MY SITUATIONS!

May 18: Praying Always

How do we grow spiritually? Winning in life is certain for those who are in constant touch with God. Praying always empowers you with the ability to do those things that are impossible for others to do. It is said that:

1. A prayerless person is powerless; a prayerful person is filled with tremendous power to activate changes in the physical and spiritual realms.

Your prayer life is constantly under attack. The enemy knows that you can change things through effective and fervent prayers. Persistent prayer of faith strengthens your whole spirit, soul, and body. Prayer matures you in spiritual and life's warfare.

Take time to pray moment by moment and schedule time to commune with God.

MEDITATION FOR THE DAY:

I WILL BE FERVENT AND CONSISTENT IN MY PRAYER LIFE IN JESUS NAME!

May 19: Speaking Mysteries

How do we grow spiritually? There are so many distractions and unknown paths that we face in our quest to fulfill our purpose on earth. We do not understand a lot of things, but through consistent praying in tongues with the help of the Holy Spirit:

1. You gain access and clarity to the deep secrets of things.
2. You energize your spirit, soul, and body; birthing in you a level of confidence to confront the issues of life.

The subject of speaking in tongues has been an arguable discussion over the years. However, the Bible is clear about one of its core purposes – "you are praying God's will, directly to Him. It allows your mind to get out of the way so your spirit can commune with the Father."

MEDITATION FOR THE DAY:

I WILL PRAY WITH UNDERSTANDING AND IN TONGUES AS THE HOLY SPIRIT EMPOWERS ME!

May 20: Share Your Story

How do we grow spiritually? Every challenge that we have been through in life presents opportunities for growth and maturity. Our stories become a source of hope and encouragement for others.

1. Telling others about how God helped you, strengthens your faith in God.
2. You empathize better with others going through difficult times in their lives.

Many of us would rather keep our hurts, pains, failures, disappointments, and even some level of success to ourselves.

The world gets better when our lives chart a path for others, bring glory to God, and keep us growing spiritually.

MEDITATION FOR THE DAY:

I WILL MAKE THE GOODNESS OF GOD IN MY LIFE KNOWN TO OTHERS!

May 21: Growth or Death

How do we grow spiritually? Everything created with life is designed for growth or it dies. Your Spirit, Soul, and Body were designed to grow, to reach your fullness of you. Growing spiritually impacts every area of your life.

1. "Physical training is good, but training for godliness is much better, promising benefits in this life and in the life to come." (1 Timothy 4:8 NLT)

The world is filled with wickedness. It is dangerous to live care-free; not being spiritually ready.

"Be on your guard and stay awake. Your enemy, the devil, is like a roaring lion, sneaking around to find someone to attack". (1 Peter 5:8 CEV)

MEDITATION FOR THE DAY:

I WILL GIVE SPIRITUAL GROWTH A PRIORITY IN MY LIFE, TODAY!

May 22: Prayer for You

Prayer changes things and enriches your spiritual growth process. "The prayer from the heart of a man right with God has much power." (James 5:16 NLV). The more prayerful you are (through the Holy Spirit), the more powerful you become.

- I yield my life to Jesus – He is my all, my Lord and Savior.
- I will study, meditate, and confess what God says in His word daily.
- I speak faith-filled words that transform situations in the name of Jesus!
- I will be fervent and consistent in my prayer life.
- I will pray with understanding and in tongues as the Holy Spirit empowers me (pray now)!
- I will make the goodness of God in my life known to others.

MEDITATION FOR THE DAY:

I WILL GIVE DAILY ATTENTION TO MY SPIRITUAL GROWTH.

May 23: Looking for Direction

There are many paths to discover, while still living on earth. Every one of us desires to be successful in academics, career, business, relationships, and where to stay or go. How do you know the right path? How do you know the will of God?

1. "If you wander from the right path, either to the right or to the left, you will hear a voice behind you saying, "You should go this way. Here is the right way." (Isaiah 30:21 ERV)

In a world filled with so much noise and distractions, it is getting difficult to cultivate the habit of seeking divine directions for our lives. We are pulled in so many directions that leaves us confused and frustrated.

You do not have to live and struggle through life being clueless, you can find the right path!

MEDITATION FOR THE DAY:

MY FATHER, SHOW ME YOUR WAYS AND TEACH ME YOUR PATH.

May 24: Desire Guidance

How do you know the right path? To know the right path starts with our desire and willingness to ask someone who knows the path. We have never lived on the face of the earth before, except for God who created the world and everything in it.

1. if you seek God, your God, you will be able to find him if you are serious, looking for him with your whole heart and soul (Deuteronomy 4:29 MSG)
2. For everyone who asks, receives. Anyone who seeks finds. If only you will knock, the door will open (Matthew 7:8)

God, your Father, knows how you can reach your goals in life. Your pursuit of Him unlocks the pathway to the all-around success you need.

Do not live your life on human suggestions, seek guidance from your all-knowing God; you will find the right path.

MEDITATION FOR THE DAY:

MY FATHER, MY SOUL THIRSTS FOR YOU, BE MY GUIDE IN JESUS' NAME.

May 25: Obey Instructions

How do you know the right path? This life contains proof that shows when we obey or disobey counsel. Many of us have experienced unusual success stories for following instructions; many others are living with the consequences of disobedience.

1. Take hold of my instructions; do not let them go. Guard them, for they are the key to life (Proverbs 4:13 NLT).

2. He who keeps instruction is in the way of life, but he who refuses correction goes astray (Proverbs 10:17 NKJV)

Obeying God's instructions and counsel from mentors helped me reset my life after a major loss. I was confused and discouraged. But all that is history.

I know the power of instructions. It will change your life and you will find the right path.

MEDITATION FOR THE DAY:

HOLY SPIRIT, FORGIVE MY DISOBEDIENCE. I WILL FOLLOW YOUR INSTRUCTIONS IN JESUS' NAME.

May 26: Be Hand-Held

How do you know the right path? The journey of life is easy to navigate if we are hand-held by someone who knows the way. The relationship we establish with such individuals gives us access to further instructions on how to reach our destination.

1. Who are those who fear the Lord? He will show them the path they should choose. (Psalms 25:12 NLT).

Do you spend time with God? Do you read and meditate on His words daily? Do you commune with Him, sharing your deepest concerns with Him? Or do you only run to Him when you are in trouble? God knows the paths to reach your goals.

Take delight in Him, build a relationship with Him and you will find the right path.

MEDITATION FOR THE DAY:

FATHER, I WANT TO GROW IN MY RELATIONSHIP WITH YOU, IN JESUS' NAME.

May 27: Horse or Mule

How do you know the right path? Knowing the right path comes with discipline and willingness to do what is expected of us. We have the free will of choice; especially the choice to yield our thoughts and desires to God's guidance.

1. Do not be like a senseless horse or mule that needs a bit and bridle to keep it under control. (Psalms 32:9 NLT).

God says, "I want to instruct you and teach you in the way you should go; I will counsel you (who are willing to learn) with my eyes upon you" (Psalms 32:8).

We cannot go far in life if we are bent on our ways. Let God guide you, and you will find the right path.

MEDITATION FOR THE DAY:

MY FATHER, I SUBMIT TO YOUR GUIDANCE AND WILL IN MY LIFE.

May 28: Put God First

How do you know the right path? Putting God first, and having absolute trust in Him, unlocks the pathway for divine direction in every area of our lives. God wants to help you; He wants to guide you and see your dreams come to pass.

1. Trust God from the bottom of your heart; do not try to figure out everything on your own (Proverbs 3:5 MSG).

2. In everything you do, put God first, and he will direct you and crown your efforts with success (Proverbs 3:6 TLB)

Sometimes I wonder why I must go through unprofitable circles before I seek God's help and direction. Living on earth can be very stress-less if we will just seek God's guidance first.

Put God first, and you will find the right path.

MEDITATION FOR THE DAY:

MY FATHER, MY GOD – I WILL SEEK YOU FIRST IN ALL MY DECISIONS.

May 29: Safety in Guidance

How do you know the right path? There are people who have been through what you are going through now. There are those who are living the dreams you and I still want to attain. You do not have to go through the tough paths of life.

1. Without good direction, people lose their way; the more wise counsel you follow, the better your chances (Proverbs 11:14 MSG).

We live in a generation where pride and self-centeredness have crippled the opportunity to seek counsel or guidance from others.

Seek guidance from others that have mastered what you are struggling with, and you will find the right path.

MEDITATION FOR THE DAY:

HOLY SPIRIT - MY GREATEST COUNSEL, GUIDE MY PATH TO WISE COUNSELS.

May 30: Receiving Divine Direction

How do you know the right path? There are so many voices out there that want to influence your decisions. Receiving direction without the help of the Holy Spirit can be frustrating and disastrous.

1. It is God's Spirit in a person, the breath of the Almighty One, that makes wise human insight possible. (Job 32:8 MSG).

To reach your desired goals, you need insight. Your human senses cannot correctly give you a clear understanding of what to do, only your human spirit, when in tune with the Holy Spirit.

Yield to the Holy Spirit today and you will find the right path.

MEDITATION FOR THE DAY:

HOLY SPIRIT – BE MY GUIDE IN THIS WORLD, IN JESUS' NAME.

May 31: You Are Not Alone

How do you know the right path? The need in our lives can become so overwhelming that the feelings of being alone in the issues seem to drown us. You wonder if there will ever be a way out or if someone even cares. God does:

1. No, I will not abandon you as orphans—I will come to you (John 14:18 NLT)
2. The Lord has promised that he will not leave us or desert us (Hebrews 13:5 CEV)

God's promises are reassuring - "Can a woman forget her nursing child, And not have compassion on the son of her womb? Surely, they may forget, Yet I will not forget you" (Isaiah 49:15 NKJV).

You will find the right path because God cares for you!

MEDITATION FOR THE DAY:

MY FATHER, I AM NOT ALONE, YOU WILL GUIDE MY PATH IN JESUS' NAME.

June 1: Prayer for You

In the beginning, God... fill in the blanks. God at the beginning of a new world brought creation to existence through His words and the working of the Holy Spirit. This month, God will...

- Show you His ways and teach you the paths to follow.
- Increase your thirst for Him and guide your ways.
- Bring healing to your heart; cause you to follow His instructions.
- Make you grow in fellowship with him.
- Teach your submission to His will and purpose for your life.
- Perfect your walk with the Holy Spirit your greatest counsel.
- Always be with you and never leave you alone.

MEDITATION FOR THE DAY:

THANK YOU, FATHER, FOR ANSWERING MY PRAYERS AND BRINGING TO PASS YOUR PROMISES IN THIS NEW MONTH, IN JESUS' NAME!

June 2: Hearing from God

The secret access to divine guidance in every area of our lives is hearing from God. This is vital to avoid wasting time, and resources and experiencing emotional constraints. Hearing from God in our noisy charged world cannot be questioned.

1. What you hear determines the quality of life you will live on earth.
2. Who you hear from determines who and what you will become in life.

We have itchy ears to hear every other thing – news, gossip, and the latest gist in town except what God is saying. Many of us have suffered disappointments in life because we do not pay attention to what God has said and is saying.

Join me in the next few days to discover how to hear from God to live a victorious life!

MEDITATION FOR THE DAY:

O LORD MY GOD, I LONG TO HEAR YOUR VOICE. TEACH ME HOW.

June 3: God Still Speaks

God still speaks, but are we listening? We are caught up in our survival mode and on the speed lane. We are so impatient to get God's perspectives about the issues of our lives. To hear God, speak to and with you, a few things must happen:

1. God will speak with you based on your relationship status with Him.
2. God will speak with you based on your priorities OR with Him.

We communicate freely and are friendly with those we have healthy relationships.

"There's a private place reserved for the lovers of God, where they sit near him and receive the revelation-secrets of his promises (Psalms 25:14 TPT)".

MEDITATION FOR THE DAY:

O LORD MY GOD, I WANT TO GROW IN LOVING AND KNOWING YOU.

June 4: Difficulty in Hearing

God wants to commune with us every moment. He wants to share deep secrets with us, guide us, instruct us on what to do, and forewarn us of dangers ahead, that you may not even know or have seen. But:

1. We have grown dull in our hearts. We have become stubborn in our way of doing things outside the instructions of God.
2. We have chosen to hear the voices, suggestions, and instructions from other sources – the media, and other humans. God is now the alternative!

"Do not be deceived, God is not mocked [He will not allow Himself to be ridiculed, nor treated with contempt nor allow His precepts to be scornfully set aside]; for whatever a man sows, this and this only is what he will reap". (Galatians 6:7 AMP)

MEDITATION FOR THE DAY:

FORGIVE ME JESUS, FOR HARDENING MY HEART TO YOU. LEAD ME IN YOUR WAYS.

June 5: Paying Attention

Another limiting factor to hearing from God is when we shut our eyes to the way we live our lives and to what happens to others. We have ignored the importance of godly character, compassion, and care for one another. We care less about others.

1. Your eyes are too pure to look on evil, and You cannot tolerate wrongdoing. (Habakkuk 1:13 Berean Bible)

It is difficult for us to share our pains and challenges with individuals we do not trust. So, it is with God.

God wants to speak with you, but you must pay attention to the things that matter to Him – then you can hear Him clearly.

MEDITATION FOR THE DAY:

FATHER, I FIX MY GAZE ON YOU. I WILL PAY ATTENTION TO WHAT MATTERS TO YOU.

June 6: In A Hurry

Oh, how we miss the opportunity to hear from God when we are in a hurry to leave the place of prayer. We remain in the dark, concerning the issues of life, when we do not spend quality time with God. Refuse the temptation to be in a rush:

1. Discipline yourself to create time to pray and commune with God.
2. It is wisdom for you to wait, to hear God's thoughts about what you have prayed about.

"Therefore, thus saith the Lord GOD, Behold, I lay in Zion for a foundation a stone, a tried stone, a precious cornerstone, a sure foundation: he that believeth shall not make haste. (Isaiah 28:16 WBT).

When you wait on God, you soar!

MEDITATION FOR THE DAY:

MY FATHER, I RECEIVE YOUR SPIRIT OF PATIENCE. I REFUSE TO BE IN A HURRY.

June 7: Hearing Advantage

The advantage we have when we hear from God, about specific matters concerning us, others, or any situation shows in the progress we make in life. We were not created to be stranded and clueless no matter the situation. Hearing from God:

1. Removes confusion, pressure, stress, and anxiety from you.
2. Sets you on the path of purpose and destiny.

When I heard God in my spirit, to stay back in my current place of residence, after a major loss (though I struggled and cried a lot), I did not know how things would turn out. I am grateful to God and to great counsel from mentors for the courage to obey.

There's a great advantage in hearing from God – don't take it for granted!

MEDITATION FOR THE DAY:

MY FATHER AND GOD, I CRAVE TO HEAR FROM YOU. SPEAK TO ME; I WILL OBEY!

June 8: Can You Hear?

The promises God has in place for you filter into your life through your eyes, heart, and ears. Your ability to take possession of these promises is in your discipline to filter the things you hear and your belief in them with your human Spirit.

1. But it is just as the Scriptures say, "What God has planned for people who love him is more than eyes have seen or ears have heard. It has never even entered our minds!" (1 Corinthians 2:9)

What God has planned for us far outweighs what our physical senses can comprehend. "But God has revealed it to us by the Spirit. The Spirit searches all things, even the deep things of God (1 Corinthians 2:10 BSB)".

Train yourself to hear from God through your spirit and your heart. The Bible is your training manual! STUDY IT!

MEDITATION FOR THE DAY:

I WILL TRAIN MY PHYSICAL SENSES TO ALIGN WITH THE WORD OF GOD.

June 9: Your Heart Listens

Most people would love to hear from God to ease the uncertainties in life. However, the way most of us expect to hear from God may never come to pass – to hear His voice with our physical ears in an audible form.

1. God speaks to your heart through your thoughts. "Be careful how you think; your life is shaped by your thoughts". (Proverbs 4:23 GNT)

You may never hear the audible voice of God in a lifetime. But you can listen with your heart and know His voice as you pray, listen to great messages, study, and meditate on His word. God speaks every day and wants to guide you with His voice.

Train your heart, to hear from God. God still speaks!

MEDITATION FOR THE DAY:

O LORD, SPEAK TO MY HEART AND I WILL LISTEN!

June 10: Quiet Whispers

The noise level in our environment can fizzle out the whispers that come with hearing from God. Our minds are flooded with thoughts, worries, and anxieties that make it difficult to filter the voice of God. To know God's voice:

Build your Trust-level with Him. Despite the noise around, you will know when He speaks because your trust is in Him.

1. Grow in your Patience-level. Resist the urge to be in a hurry. Through patience, you master every life situation

2. Strengthen your Obedience-level to what He says to you.

To hear God's voice and direction in life is your guaranteed ticket to continually fly in every area of life.

MEDITATION FOR THE DAY:

MY GOD, I TRUST IN YOU. I WILL WAIT ON YOU AND OBEY YOUR INSTRUCTIONS.

June 11: Prayer for You

One day Jesus told his disciples a story to show that they should always pray and never give up (Luke 18:1 NLT). Today, I encourage you not to allow challenges to weaken your desire to pray. Your answers are locked up in your prayer of faith.

- My Father forgives my disobedience. I will follow your path.
- My God, teach me to grow in loving and knowing you more.
- My Father, I long to hear your voice. Speak to my heart.
- I receive your grace to align my physical senses with your words.
- My Father, speak to my heart concerning the issues of my life.
- My God, I trust you. I will wait on you and obey your instructions.

MEDITATION FOR THE DAY:

FATHER, THANK YOU FOR BRINGING ME ANSWERS WITH SPEED, IN JESUS' NAME!

June 12: Exploits

The word EXPLOIT has several meanings and interpretations that express the potentials and abilities that God has given to us, to excel while we are still living in this world. But the way the trouble of life weakens us – worries me.

1. You have been created to make full use of and to derive the benefits of all that God created.
2. You were created with the daring, bold, and fearless nature of God.

God wants you to leave a footprint on the earth. "For all creation, gazing eagerly as if with an outstretched neck, is waiting and longing to see the manifestation of the sons of God (Romans 8:19 WNT)".

You cannot manifest or become relevant, except you are making exploits!

MEDITATION FOR THE DAY:

I AM CREATED FOR EXPLOITS!

June 13: Know Your God

The knowledge of God and our relationship with him determines the level of exploits we can achieve. God has countless stories of exploits since the creation of the world. You are made in His image – making exploits are in your DNA

1. "…but the people that do know their God shall be strong and do exploits (Daniel 11:32b KJV)".

You cannot take life as it is or as it comes. You have a mandate to "be fruitful and multiply. Fill the earth and govern it (Genesis 1:28 NLT)". I challenge you today, to give growth in the knowledge of God a priority in your life.

The knowledge of God gives you access to the keys to making exploits in every area of your life!

MEDITATION FOR THE DAY:

HOLY SPIRIT, FILL ME WITH THE PASSION TO KNOW MY FATHER AND MY GOD DAILY.

June 14: Self-Knowledge

The greatest exploit we can achieve in life is having deep self-knowledge of who we are and whose we are. When you realize this, the world turns into your playground, you chart the course of your life through God's eyes.

1. "...because the Spirit who is in you is more powerful than the spirit in those who belong to the world (1 John 4:4 GNT)".

Your exploits – in career, relationships, business, health, and finances are hinged on who you think you are, your capabilities, and above all, the God whom you re-image.

I am in the euphoria that my exploits come from who I am in God. What about you?

MEDITATION FOR THE DAY:

I HAVE BEEN SO AMAZINGLY AND MIRACULOUSLY MADE. I AM MADE FOR EXPLOITS!

June 15: See Possibilities

To achieve great feats in life starts with what you see in your imagination. Our physical world is designed to bring into reality the thoughts we conceptualize in the fourth dimension (the realm of spiritual creations). What do you see?

1. Never allow what you see with your physical eyes or what your environment presents to be the driving force of your life. You can change what you see

2. The forces that drive our physical world are unseen. You are a vessel for the greatest force that controls the universe.

You have been created to live on the first dimension (physical plane) and given the authority to operate from the fourth dimension (the spiritual plane). Life exploits are determined in the spiritual plane.

See possibilities - you can achieve great feats!

MEDITATION FOR THE DAY:

I CAN DO ALL THINGS THROUGH CHRIST BECAUSE HE GIVES ME STRENGTH!

June 16: Can-Do-Spirit

Every human being has been given the can-do spirit! But the fear of the unknown, the negative experiences of the past, and the mindset of 'what if I fail?' has weakened our abilities to accomplish what is in our destinies. Hear this:

1. "...Anything is possible if a person believes (Mark 9:23 NLT)". Do you believe it?
2. "If you fall to pieces in a crisis, there wasn't much to you in the first place (Proverbs 24:10 MSG)".

Life gives you what you demand from it no matter what you have been through or going through. God has designed you to be in command of life circumstances with His help. One of Henry Ford's greatest quotes says: "Whether you think you can or can't, either way, you are right".

But I know YOU CAN!

MEDITATION FOR THE DAY:

I CAN DO ALL THINGS THROUGH CHRIST BECAUSE HE GIVES ME STRENGTH!

June 17: It's in You

Do you feel like giving up because things are not working out as you expect? Do you feel left out, downcast, and powerless because of the countless failures and disappointments? Does God seem so far away, and your cries neglected?

1. "No test or temptation that comes your way is beyond the course of what others have had to face. All you need to remember is that God will never let you down; he will never let you be pushed past your limit; he'll always be there to help you come through it. (1 Corinthians 10:13 MSG)"

The challenges of life have a way of blurring our minds from the exploits and adventures we have ahead. You have got what it takes to break free from every limiting factor.

Arise! Shine! Your light has come (Isaiah 60:1 GW)

MEDITATION FOR THE DAY:

I MAKE EXPLOITS; CHRIST LIVES IN ME!

June 18: Words and Exploits

The speech center of the human brain has been identified as a critical success factor in the happenings in our lives. It governs the outcome of our state of well-being, and overall exploits in life. In other words, YOUR WORDS MOVE YOUR LIFE!

1. "...we understand that the worlds were framed by the word of God, so that the things which are seen were not made of things which are visible. (Hebrews 11:3 NKV)"
2. Remember the war of words between David and Goliath? (1 Samuel 17:43-47)

Spoken words are raw materials to frame the future and exploit you desire. You cannot be victorious by speaking fearful, weak, and discouraging words about yourself or situations. Your words carry life.

Say what you want to see!

MEDITATION FOR THE DAY:

MY WORDS SHAPE MY FUTURE IN CHRIST JESUS!

June 19: Power for Exploits

The earth was in chaos before creation took place. God, through the Holy Spirit, spoke and the earth gained form. Man, since then has been involved in great exploits – discovering medicine, technologies, constructions, and much more!

1. The exploits you were made to achieve are inside of you. You have got the power!
2. God has crowned you with glory and honor. You were made for GLORY!

God's greatest pain is the unfulfilled YOU! You must not go through life without living to the fullness of your potential.

Make exploits, discover what ignites your passion, and go all out to make God proud!

MEDITATION FOR THE DAY:

I RECEIVE THE POWER OF THE HOLY SPIRIT TO MAKE EXPLOITS IN LIFE!

June 20: Exploits Partner

The journey to exploit can be lonely and scary. The steps to take, the paths to follow, the people to talk to, and the final decision, never comes with ease. These moments define the depth of your exploits. Just remember, you are not alone:

1. And I will ask the Father, and He will give you another Helper (Comforter, Advocate, Intercessor—Counselor, Strengthener, Standby), to be with you forever (John 14:16 Amplified Version)

Friends, you are not supposed to go through life alone. Humans will always fail, but God has given you a trusted partner – The Holy Spirit. The Holy Spirit wants to help you, guide you, strengthen you, and lead you into unspeakable exploits.

Open your heart, and life to Him (The Holy Spirit) now!

MEDITATION FOR THE DAY:

HOLY SPIRIT, I NEED YOU IN MY LIFE. I DEPEND ON YOU FOR EXPLOITS IN LIFE.

June 21: Prayer for You

I can guarantee this truth: This is what will be done for someone who doesn't doubt but believes what he says will happen: He can say to this mountain, 'Be uprooted and thrown into the sea,' and it will be done for him (Mark 11:23 GWT).

- I have been so amazingly and miraculously made. I am made for exploits!
- I can do all things through Christ because He gives me strength!
- I make exploits daily; Christ lives in me!
- My words shape my future in Christ Jesus!
- I receive the power of the Holy Spirit to make exploits in life!

MEDITATION FOR THE DAY:

HOLY SPIRIT, I NEED YOU IN MY LIFE. I DEPEND ON YOU FOR EXPLOITS IN LIFE.

June 22: Endless Love

One of the greatest R&B songs that I loved so much during my late elementary, and most parts of my high school days was "Endless Love", by Dianna Ross and Lionel Richie. The song formed most of our 'language' for wooing any sweet girl we admired (lol). Are you feeling lost in matters of love in our love-less world?

1. God's love for you is endless. "I love you with an everlasting love. So, I will continue to show you my kindness (Jeremiah 31:3 GWT)"

We struggle every day on the issue of love – for others, for ourselves, and especially for God. We were created to love and to be loved.

The big questions are: where did we miss it? How did we allow love to become skewed in our hearts and world today?

MEDITATION FOR THE DAY:

THANK YOU, FATHER, FOR LOVING ME ENDLESSLY.

June 23: Father's Love

Everyone born of a woman has a father. But the uncertainties of life and our human weaknesses have deprived many of us of the love, care, and nurturing of our earthly fathers. This may have had some impact on your struggles with relationships with people and making concrete progress in life. Be encouraged. How?

1. What marvelous love the Father has extended to us! Just look at it—we are called children of God! That is who we really are (1 John 3:1 MSG).

There is no doubt that the love of our earthly father means so much to us. But the love of God is pure and unconditional. In God, your healing is restored, and your destiny is secured. God's love gave us Jesus and the Holy Spirit to help us experience love again.

Open your heart again – God loves you beyond words.

MEDITATION FOR THE DAY:

THANK YOU, FATHER, FOR LOVING ME UNCONDITIONALLY.

June 24: First Love

There are different levels at which we experience the embrace of love. The love of a mother at birth, the love from family, our first relationship with the opposite sex, and marriage. But your true first love is God. His love comes with a great plan:

1. "I knew you before you were formed within your mother's womb; before you were born I sanctified you and appointed you as my spokesman to the world." (Jeremiah 1:5 TLB)

God formed and loved us for His purpose. We cannot thrive in human relationships without giving God the first place in our lives. He wants you to share fellowship, love, and grow in your knowledge of Him daily.

Express your love to God today.

MEDITATION FOR THE DAY:

MY FATHER, THANK YOU FOR YOUR LOVE FOR ME. HELP ME TO GROW IN LOVING YOU AND HUMANITY.

June 25: Incapable of Loving

In my quest to love, and to be loved as a teenager until my adulthood, I thought I could love unconditionally. In hindsight, most of my love has been conditional. I show more love when the other person is responsive to my needs, I become indifferent when the conditions do not favor me. God wants you to:

1. "Love from the center of who you are; don't fake it." (Romans 12:9 MSG)

We can be hypocritical with our claims of true love for others. Without the help of the Holy Spirit and the love of God, we are incapable of loving without conditions. Open your heart today and ask the Holy Spirit to share within you the kind of love that Christ showed to humanity.

You can love genuinely – YES YOU CAN!

MEDITATION FOR THE DAY:

HOLY SPIRIT LET YOUR FOUNTAIN OF LOVE, FLOW IN MY LIFE, IN JESUS' NAME!

June 26: Love Expression

The expression of love is an act of the state of our hearts. We express love by how we feel most of the time, and not by what we do. Love is expressed through action, not through feeling. In a statement, love expresses itself through self-sacrifice:

1. "The greatest way to show love for friends is to die for them." (John 15:13 CEV)

The scripture above is scary! Die for my friends? For real? (lol). The expression of our love for people goes beyond words. "… let us stop just saying we love people; let us love them and show it by our actions". (1 John 3:18 TLB).

Respect the feelings of others, honor them, provide moral and spiritual support when you can, empathize, and learn to forgive! All of these have a way of coming back to you!

MEDITATION FOR THE DAY:

HOLY SPIRIT, GIVE ME YOUR KIND OF LOVE FOR PEOPLE AND MYSELF.

June 27: Love Hurts Sometimes

Most acts of human endeavors and expressions involve sacrifice. One such is LOVE. As beautiful and sweet as the act of love is, it hurts sometimes. Love is about giving and receiving. But when taken advantage of, it hurt so bad! Despite the hurt:

1. "Love never gives up, never loses faith, is always hopeful, and endures through every circumstance". (1 Corinthians 13:7 NLT)

I am not advocating for the tolerance of abusive and destructive love, but sometimes there's God's saving grace comeback for the most love-hurt situation. We must be ready to experience the hurts that come with loving!

MEDITATION FOR THE DAY:

HOLY SPIRIT, GIVE ME YOUR KIND OF LOVE FOR PEOPLE AND MYSELF.

June 28: Love Heals

No doubt that the hurts, pains, and disappointments we experience from a lost, stressed, and abusive relationship (s) are unbearable. So many people have lost their minds, self-esteem, happiness, and even their lives. No human soothing words or actions may restore us. But the greatest love on earth can heal and restore you:

1. "The Spirit of the Lord is upon me... he has sent me to heal the broken hearted". (Luke 4:18 TLB).

Jesus is God's love sent to us, to bring healing to our love-struck hearts! His love heals beyond words and actions. I have had first-hand experience with this. The recovery process is tough and wrapped with uncertainties. But the love of Jesus will heal every fiber of your body, soul, and spirit.

Open your heart to Him (Jesus Christ) today.

MEDITATION FOR THE DAY:

HOLY SPIRIT, HEAL MY BROKEN HEART. I WANT TO LOVE AS YOU DO.

June 29: Love Demands

Loving is no joke. It comes with great sacrifice and commitment to others. To love is to be "selfless and others-full". This comes with a high level of demand that we need grace and maturity to handle.

1. 4 "Love is patient and kind. Love is not jealous or boastful or proud 5 or rude. It does not demand its own way. It is not irritable, and it keeps no record of being wrong........ 7 Love never gives up, never loses faith, is always hopeful, and endures through every circumstance." (1 Corinthians 13:4-7 NLT)

To love others, we must be ready and willing to put in the work. We will be vulnerable, our time demanded, and our resources invested.

Loving others is your nature from your Father – God!

MEDITATION FOR THE DAY: HOLY SPIRIT, I RECEIVE YOUR GRACE TO HANDLE THE DEMANDS OF LOVING OTHERS, IN JESUS' NAME!

June 30: Love Code

The existence of humans has its bedrock built on love. Without it, our fights will be worse than the shark fights that turn the blue ocean into a red ocean! Christ gave us the love code in Matthew 22:37-40 (The Passion Translation):

1. 37 "'Love the Lord your God with every passion of your heart, with all the energy of your being, and with every thought that is within you.........
    39 And the second is like it in importance: 'You must love your friend in the same way you love yourself.' 40 Contained within these commandments to love you will find all the meaning of the Law and the Prophets."

These two commandments will change your life forever!

I pray that God will give you uncommon grace to live by His Love Code, in Jesus' name!

MEDITATION FOR THE DAY:

HOLY SPIRIT, HELP ME TO LIVE BY YOUR LOVE INSTRUCTIONS, IN JESUS' NAME!

July 1: Prayer for You

In the beginning, God... fill in the blanks. God at the beginning of a new world brought creation to existence through His words and the working of the Holy Spirit. This month, God will:

- Show you His ways and teach you the paths to follow.
- Increase your thirst for Him and guide your ways.
- Bring healing to your heart; cause you to follow His instructions.
- Make you grow in fellowship with Him.
- Teach you submission to His will and purpose for your life.
- Perfect your walk with the Holy Spirit your greatest counsel.
- Always be with you and never leave you alone.

MEDITATION FOR THE DAY:

FATHER, THANK YOU FOR ANSWERING MY PRAYERS AND BRINGING TO PASS YOUR PROMISES TO ME IN THE MONTH OF JUNE, IN JESUS' NAME!

July 2: Hearing from God

The secret access to divine guidance in every area of our lives is hearing from God. This is vital to avoid wasting time, and resources and experiencing emotional constraints. Hearing from God in our noisy charged world cannot be questioned.

1. What you hear determines the quality of life you will live on earth.
2. Who you hear from determines who and what you will become in life.

We have itchy ears to hear every other thing – news, gossip, and the latest gist in town except what God is saying. Many of us have suffered disappointments in life because we do not pay attention to what God has said and is saying.

Join me in the next few days to discover how to hear from God to live a victorious life!

MEDITATION FOR THE DAY:

O LORD MY GOD, I LONG TO HEAR YOUR VOICE. TEACH ME HOW.

July 3: Is God Alive?

The magnitude of the challenges we face in life, and the increase of evil in our world have pushed many of us to the point of questioning the existence of God. We have laid the blames for our failures and shortcomings on God. However:

1. Questioning the existence of God shows that He exists.
2. The issues going on in your life and the increase of wickedness in our world are not His choices but ours.

God is sovereign, loving, compassionate, and kind. He knows all that is going on in your life and our world. But He cannot break His code of ethics in the governance of our lives and world. "The heavens belong to our God; they are his alone, but he has given us the earth and put us in charge." (Psalms 115:16).

Yes, God is alive! Yield to God's governing code – His word!

MEDITATION FOR THE DAY: MY FATHER AND GOD, YOU LIVE AND REIGN FOREVER. I YIELD TO YOUR GOVERNING CODE.

July 4: God is Wicked

You had everything going on for you – a great career, lovely relationships, financial prosperity, and within a split moment, you lost a child, and a spouse, and experienced a downturn in finances, career, health, and relationships; and the troubles would not go away. How could God allow these to happen? Many of us usually conclude that God is wicked, heartless, and merciless. Is He not God? Where was He?

Really? The nature and character of God can never be seen with a trace of our human assumptions and conclusions when the storms of life hit us. King David understood this: "For You are not a God who takes pleasure in wickedness" (Psalms 5:4).

In God, there is no wickedness. His love exceeds the pains and challenges you will ever go through. Repent today; experience His goodness.

MEDITATION FOR THE DAY:

MY FATHER, I REPENT FROM MY WRONG CONCLUSIONS ABOUT YOU. YOU'RE A GOOD FATHER; I'M LOVED BY YOU.

July 5: There is no God

A celebrated scientist, who died at the age of 76years, concluded in his book, which was published after his death: "There is no God. No one directs the universe". He insisted that science can explain the universe without the need for a creator. But surprisingly, he had a few concerns before his death:

1. How divided we have become. How we seem to have lost the ability to look outward, and we are increasingly looking inward at ourselves.
2. How can we shape the future? The scientist wrote: "Remember to look up at the stars and not down at your feet."

The answers to his concerns are clearly documented in God's word. The answers to the troubles of humanity cannot be found in any being but in God.

I believe strongly that there is a God. Do you believe it?

MEDITATION FOR THE DAY: I BELIEVE IN GOD – THE HEAVEN IS HIS THRONE; THE EARTH, HIS FOOT-STOOL AND HE LIVES IN ME!

July 6: Foolishness of God

We live in an era where several human movements, ideologies, beliefs, and systems are showcasing how wiser, smarter, and more intelligent they are than God. We have accepted the craftiness of these philosophies, that we can live our lives outside the principles of the God who created the universe.

1. Even when God is foolish, he is wiser than everyone else, and even when God is weak, he is stronger than everyone else. (1 Corinthians 1:25 CEV)

2. For the wisdom of this world is foolishness to God. As the Scriptures say, "He traps the wise in the snare of their own cleverness. (1 Corinthians 3:19 NLT)

The wisest of us, smartest of us, and most intelligent of us can never compare with the foolishness of God (He can never be foolish). Let your life be controlled by the concepts and principles of God.

MEDITATION FOR THE DAY: THANK YOU, FATHER, FOR CHOOSING THE FOOLISH AND WEAK OVER THE WISE AND POWERFUL!

July 7: Does God Exist?

The existence of God remains a subject that over 70% of the world's population doubts. Atheists and scientific cultures believe that 'the universe is just eternal and uncaused'. They argue that the universe began existing in a great explosion called the Big Bang fifteen billion years ago. But countless pieces of evidence show that God exists:

1. The complexity of our planet points to a deliberate Designer who not only created our universe but sustains it today. (everystudent.com)
2. We know God exists because He pursues us. He is constantly initiating and seeking for us to come to him. (everystudent.com)

Are there issues in life that you are going through, which are challenging the existence of God? They exist because there is a God who can resolve them for you. Are you breathing right now?

That is the existence of God!

MEDITATION FOR THE DAY:

MY GOD, MY FATHER, I BELIEVE IN YOUR EXISTENCE AND YOU LIVE IN ME!

July 8: Knowledge Against God

The increase in human discoveries in the areas of science, technology, and social evolution has developed an unprecedented disregard for the existence of God. We think everything we have achieved is the sole product of our minds and not God's.

1. No wisdom, no understanding, and no counsel will prevail against the LORD. (Proverbs 21:30 CSB)
2. No one can do anything unless God in heaven allows it. (John 3:27 CEV)

Our human knowledge is flawed without the approval and consent of God. In all that we seek to achieve in life, they must fit into the grand design of God's purposes.

We are in great distress today, because of our superior claim of knowledge, above God.

MEDITATION FOR THE DAY:

MY GOD, MY FATHER, I ACKNOWLEDGE YOUR SUPERIOR KNOWLEDGE OVER HUMAN KNOWLEDGE!

July 9: God Exists

Friends, strap your seat belt, as I would love to ask some questions about some things in our world; then you can make your conclusions if God exists or not. See questions from a conversation between God and Job:

1. Where were you when the foundation of the earth was laid?

2. Who determined the measurements (of the earth) if you know?

3. Since your days began, have you ever commanded the morning, and caused the dawn to know its place?

4. Have you ever entered and explored the springs of the sea or (have you) walked in the recesses of the deep?

5. Have the gates of death been revealed to you, or have you seen the gates of deep darkness?

Dear friends, do you have answers to the above questions? Can God 's critics provide answers to them?

We will more questions tomorrow.

MEDITATION FOR THE DAY:

MY GOD, MY FATHER, I SEE THE WONDERS OF YOUR CREATION!

July 10: Matchless Creator

The existence of a creator is not in doubt. But who is this creator of all that exists? Have you found answers to the questions of yesterday? Some more questions to think through:

1. Where does light come from, and where does darkness go?
2. Have you visited the storehouses of the snow or seen the storehouses of hail?
3. Who sends rain to satisfy the parched ground and make the tender grass spring up?
4. Who gives intuition to the heart and instinct to the mind?
5. Do you know when wild goats give birth? Have you watched as deer are born in the wild? (Job 38 and 39)

Only a matchless creator – God, who exists, and lives in you by His Holy Spirit. Only a fool can say, "there's no God"! Do you still doubt the existence of God?

MEDITATION FOR THE DAY:

MY GOD, I BELIEVE YOU EXIST AND HAVE EVERYTHING IN YOUR CONTROL!

July 11: Prayer for You

We reflect who and what we believe. The existence of God and the acknowledgment of His sovereignty over the universe and humanity influence us. Your life's outcomes are hinged on you believing that God exists.

- I believe in the existence of God, and He has control over all.
- Thank you for choosing the weak to confound the mighty.
- I acknowledge the superior knowledge of God over human knowledge.
- I believe in the wonders of God's creation – I am uniquely created for Him!

MEDITATION FOR THE DAY:

I AM THE EXPRESS IMAGE OF GOD – HE REIGNS AND LIVES IN ME!

July 12: Making a Comeback

Life is full of uncertainties. Experiencing an unexpected loss of a job, or family member, displacement, sickness, and relationships (especially an early or long-time marriage) can be devastating. Many of us find it very difficult to regain our positions.

1. Questions, thoughts, flashbacks, and fear of the future grip you.
2. The struggles on how to move on coupled with the fear of the unknown greet you daily.

This life is full of trials, challenges, pains, and hurts that will snuff out the best of you. I lost it when sickness took a dear one away from me.

How did I survive those dark days? How did I make a comeback to live a life in pursuit of God's purposes?

MEDITATION FOR THE DAY:

MY GOD, I THANK YOU FOR MY COMEBACK FROM LIFE'S CHALLENGES!

July 13: How Do I Survive?

When the pressures and sudden heartbreaks of life take hold of us, one of the questions we ask is: how do I survive this? How do I live without a loved one? How do I take care of my family? How do I meet the mounting needs? (How? How? How?)

1. As best you can, do not let what happened to you redefine who God is. God will give you a comeback if you allow Him.
2. You have been created to survive and overcome any adversity in life.

Everything that happens to you either brings out the best or worst in you. You must make a conscious effort to fix your gaze on the Holy Spirit.

He alone (The Holy Spirit) and the people he sends your path, can help you survive and thrive through all difficult situations.

MEDITATION FOR THE DAY:

I CAN SURVIVE AND THRIVE IN ALL THINGS, THROUGH CHRIST JESUS!

July 14: Where do I go?

The sudden obstruction to the natural workings of our relationships, finances, health, career, and purpose in life, has a way of bringing doubts, uncertainties, and the fear of the unknown. We are moved to ask, "where do I go from here?"

1. Everything you have dreamt of, thought about, wished for, and aspired to achieve becomes a mirage.

2. The only way out of the dark path is to call on Him – who knows how to navigate the darkest seasons of your life.

During these seasons of our lives, day and night become longer, we lose the essence of living, and the drive for what we love fades out. But you can have a comeback! As the nights go darker, God's light and help come brighter.

I encourage you to open your heart to His Life-Giving Spirit – The Holy Spirit.

MEDITATION FOR THE DAY: HOLY SPIRIT, LEAD ME THROUGH MY DARK NIGHTS, IN JESUS' NAME.

July 15: I am Done!

The excitement of a new relationship, career, new opportunities, and new births can be indescribable. The hopes, expectations, and dreams can turn in sharp contrast when things fall apart. As divorce, separation, death, disappointments, failures, and retrenchment take their hold, all you just want to say is, "I am done"! Hear Jesus:

1. "...Here on earth you will have many trials and sorrows. But take heart, because I have overcome the world." (John 16:33)

You cannot be done when life seems to turn the table against you. Every setback in your life is God's set-up for the next phase of His purposes for you. Look unto Jesus, seek the Holy Spirit for His help and will.

Your comeback is certain in God!

MEDITATION FOR THE DAY:

I REFUSE TO GIVE UP ON MYSELF. I LOOK UNTO JESUS – MY HOPE AND RESTORER!

July 16: Where Did I Go Wrong?

The emotions that wrap us around when the unexpected happens erupt so many questions in our heart. As best as you can, you want to take a critical and objective look at the situation and never stop asking yourself, "where did I go wrong"?

1. This question can and will put a heavy weight and burden upon your already heavy heart.
2. Asking 'what did I do wrong? Can keep you in a lost world of endless regrets and pains.

It is human to place quick judgment on oneself when things go the wrong way. Most times it is not about what you did or did not do!

Life plays its cards the painful way, but you can always have your comeback because God has got your back!

MEDITATION FOR THE DAY:

HOLY SPIRIT, THANK YOU FOR BEING THERE FOR ME!

July 17: What Do I Do?

When your back is against the wall, and it looks as if everything in your life is over, what do you do? The dreams, the expectations, the hopes, and the faith you once had – are dashed into pieces; your heart never seeks to ask, 'what do I do?'

1. What to do, may not come so easy with the swiftness you expect.
2. My sincere counsel - Wait on God. He knows what you should do.

Waiting on God can be hard. You want to forget the pains, hurts, disappointments, and failures. But how? "… those who trust the Lord will find new strength. They will be strong like eagles soaring upward on wings; they will walk and run without getting tired. (Isaiah 40:31 CEV)".

I encourage you to depend on the Holy Spirit. He knows all things!

MEDITATION FOR THE DAY:

HOLY SPIRIT, I WILL WAIT ON YOU FOR MY COMEBACK!

July 18: Encourage Yourself

Life presents countless circumstances that make the impact of pain, hurt, failures, and disappointments inevitable, yet excruciating. Many will come as no fault of yours. But you must decide if what happened will mar or make you.

1. "David was seriously worried, for in their bitter grief for their children, his men began talking of killing him. But David took strength from the Lord. (1 Samuel 30:6)"

When all chips are down – the loss of a loved one, job or career, relationship, failure, or disappointment, we must embrace them and take strength in God.

External support is good, but strength from within through the help of the Holy Spirit is what will see you through to your comeback!

MEDITATION FOR THE DAY:

HOLY SPIRIT, I DEPEND ON YOUR GRACE AND STRENGTH IN JESUS' NAME!

July 19: Lord Save Me!

Who do we turn to when things fall apart in our lives? Fellow humans? Mediums? Occult powers? Self-righteousness? Blame game? Or even commit suicide? When things fall apart, you can count on Him who makes all things work for your good.

1. Seek God and call upon Him. He knows the path to your comeback.
2. Take the bold step to do what He has asked you to do.

It is wisdom to run to God instead of running away from Him. He has given countless individuals a comeback from bitter situations in their lives. I know He will give you a comeback from whatever you are passing through right now!

Seek Him (God), depend on the Holy Spirit and take that bold step He has asked you to take!

MEDITATION FOR THE DAY:

THANK YOU, JESUS, MY COMEBACK IS SURE!

July 20: Nothing is Impossible

When we go through those painful and hurtful experiences, life can become almost impossible to live. You lose meaning in the things you once loved, nothing excites you anymore, and all you just want to do is give up!

1. Do not give up, friend! Your life is still important to millions of people waiting to hear how you had your great comeback

2. Your comeback is not impossible. "For with God nothing will be impossible." (Luke 1:37 NKJV)

Your pains, hurts, failures, and disappointments are shaping your message, and God's purposes for your life. The pains you go through are the pleasures God uses to make the beauty of your life an example to others!

Your comeback is sure, hold on!

MEDITATION FOR THE DAY:

THANK YOU, JESUS, NOTHING IS IMPOSSIBLE WITH YOU – EVEN MY COMEBACK!

July 21: Prayer for You

God can give you a comeback. God can turn your deepest pains into pleasure. "You have turned my mourning into dancing for me; You have taken off my sackcloth and clothed me with joy (Psalms 30:11)."

- My God, thank you for my comeback from life's challenges.
- I thrive in all things through Christ Jesus!
- I refuse to give up, my eyes are on Jesus Christ – my hope and restorer!
- Holy Spirit, I depend on your grace and strength in Jesus' name!

MEDITATION FOR THE DAY:

THANK YOU, JESUS, FOR MY COMEBACK!

July 22: Attitude

The Merriam-Webster dictionary gave two remarkable definitions of the meaning of the word "ATTITUDE":

1. a mental position with regard to a fact or state
2. a feeling or emotion toward a fact or state

Wow! As humans, we are faced with different facts about life and the state of how things are in our lives. But it is pertinent to note that these facts or states of things are not as strong as our mental position about them. What you are thinking, the emotions you hold about your life, and all that is going on around you are all that matter.

What is your attitude about what you are going through?

MEDITATION FOR THE DAY:

MY ATTITUDE IS CONTROLLED BY MY MENTAL POSITION IN CHRIST!

July 23: Mental Attitude

The lion is not the largest, smartest, or strongest animal in the jungle, but it remains the king of the jungle. The mental attitude of the lion towards other animals and the attitude of other animals towards the lion makes the difference.

1. The state of your mind towards the challenges in your life determines the results you will get.
2. What you see with the eyes of your mind is what your reality will eventually become.

Remember the story of David in the Bible? His mental attitude toward the size of Goliath made all the difference. Others were seeing a giant and a terror, but David saw meat for the birds of the air. What is your mental attitude toward your challenges?

We will always get what we see and believe with our mind's eyes!

MEDITATION FOR THE DAY:

I SEE POSSIBILITIES AND VICTORIES IN EVERY AREA OF MY LIFE!

July 24: Emotional Attitude

The strain and stress we experience in relationships –
marriage, business, courtship, work, and other areas of
our lives, come from the state of our emotional attitude.
We lack emotional intelligence on how to relate with
others and how to manage the challenges we face.

1. One of the habits of highly effective people is to,
   "seek first to understand, then to be understood"
   - (Steven Covey)
2. A soft and gentle and thoughtful answer turns
   away wrath, but harsh and painful, and careless
   words stir up anger. (Proverbs 15:1 AMP)

The power of emotional attitude is put to the test in
relationships. Your maturity is tested by the way you
handle the emotions of anger, love, guilt, grief,
displeasure, disappointment, and so on.

Your life is played out in the way you handle your
emotions!

MEDITATION FOR THE DAY:

I YIELD MY EMOTIONS TO THE CONTROL OF
THE HOLY SPIRIT, IN JESUS' NAME!

July 25: Physical Attitude

Our outward appearance reflects our mental position regarding our physical posture. Many who take time to exercise, eat well, and get some rest, have increased chances to boost their confidence and appearance. Even God recognizes this:

1. As the saying goes, "Exercise is good for your body... (1 Timothy 4:8 CEV)
2. Exercise daily in God—no spiritual flabbiness, please! Workouts in the gymnasium are useful (1 Timothy 4:8 MSG)

The wealth, success, and power we all seek, can only be meaningful if we have a healthy, and stable physical body to enjoy or appreciate them.

Give attention to your physical well-being – God needs your body for His purposes on earth!

MEDITATION FOR THE DAY:

I WILL GIVE ATTENTION TO MY PHYSICAL BODY, AS I GROW SPIRITUALLY.

July 26: Financial Attitude

Financial attitude has to do with our mental position concerning 'Money' and how to increase it. How we get money, the abundance of it, the scarcity of it, and how we put it to work or hoard it, is an offshoot of our attitude.

1.   You may never increase your capacity to create wealth or earn a good income if your mental position about money is limited or flawed.

God has designed life for increase and productivity. If you think of lack and scarcity, you will get lack and scarcity. If your thought is filled with abundance and more than enough money to make, you will attract God's idea on how to increase your capacity to be productive.

Your finances depend on your attitude!

MEDITATION FOR THE DAY:

THERE IS MORE THAN ENOUGH FOR ME, IN CHRIST JESUS!

July 27: Spiritual Attitude

The successes of other areas of attitudes (Mental, Emotional, Physical and Financial) thrive when we have a healthy Spiritual Attitude. A spiritual attitude means choosing to follow a path that is inspired by love, kindness, wisdom, and other virtues that lead to a better world. (Google search). But how do you cultivate this attitude?

1. But when the Holy Spirit controls our lives he will produce this kind of fruit in us: love, joy, peace, patience, kindness, goodness, faithfulness, gentleness, and self-control... (Galatians 5:22-23 TLB)

A life controlled by the Holy Spirit produces a great spiritual attitude. My quest daily is to allow the Holy Spirit to influence, control, and energize my words, thoughts, and actions.

Will you allow the Holy Spirit to do the same with you daily?

MEDITATION FOR THE DAY:

MY LIFE IS CONTROLLED, INFLUENCED, AND ANIMATED BY THE HOLY SPIRIT!

July 28: Attitude and Belief

Truly, attitude is the position of our mental and emotional state. However, attitude is played out, based on what is registered in our mental and emotional faculties. You and I can never rise above the state of our attitudes.

1. Your attitude feeds on what your belief is, about you and others.
2. Your belief determines how far you will go in life and your relationships.

The way you see things is the way you are inside. The way you act or respond to situations reflects the attitude of your beliefs. The way you say things shows the state of your mental and emotional positioning.

What do you believe in?

MEDITATION FOR THE DAY:

AS I THINK SO AM I. HENCE, MY BELIEFS MUST ALIGN WITH WHAT GOD THINKS!

July 29: Attitude: Stinks or Scents

Our mental and emotional state produces an aroma that is either a sweet scent or a foul stink. You are attracted to people because of your attitude to life and the maturity of your mental and emotional state.

1. Your attitude reveals your motives, your motives show who you are.
2. Who you are attracts the quality of those who want to come around you!

Your attitude is powerful. It is wrapped up in your personal magnet. It determines the course of your life. Do not trade anything for the development of a positive attitude.

Your attitude is what keeps you standing and relevant through ticks and thorns!

MEDITATION FOR THE DAY:

HOLY SPIRIT, INFLUENCE MY ATTITUDE FOR YOUR GLORY!

July 30: Test of Attitude

Our attitude on how we respond to the challenges and circumstances we encounter will be tested for maturity and growth. When things do not go your way, how do you process or respond in your mental and emotional state?

1. Separate the issues and situations from personal (you, others, or the situation) faults and take a bird's eye view of the issues.
2. Make a personal decision to grow through the challenges, become the best of yourself, and have a godly perspective about the issues.

Your claim of maturity and positive mental state will be tested. But this is your winning key: "You, therefore, will be perfect [growing into spiritual maturity both in mind and character, actively integrating godly values into your daily life], as your heavenly Father is perfect" (Matthew 5:48 AMP).

MEDITATION FOR THE DAY:

HOLY SPIRIT, MAKE ME MORE LIKE JESUS – IN WORDS, THOUGHTS, AND ACTIONS!

July 31: Prayer for You

We have been made for more, to live a life of victory. However, crises, troubles, challenges, and unpleasant circumstances are drivers that test our attitude, character, and maturity. As July ends, I pray that:

- Your trials and temptations shall become your testimonies.
- Your painful circumstances shall turn out to bring you pleasurable moments.
- Your sorrows turn to Joy.

MEDITATION FOR THE DAY:

MY MOURNING HAS TURNED INTO DANCING AGAIN!

August 1: Time – Your Essence

Happy new month my dear friends! Thank you for being part of Everyday Fragrance. It is a journey that is birthed by God's idea, and I pray it continually be a great blessing to you. Thank you for sharing with others.

1. The subject of time, its usage, its purpose, and its advantage are a long age discourse. But it's effect on you cannot be quantified if not managed.
2. Time is the essence of your life. The mastery of it is your access to unlimited success in life.

Take these quick short prayers for victories in August:

I will live to fulfill God's plans for my life!

I will be the best of me this month, in Jesus' name!

MEDITATION FOR THE DAY:

LORD JESUS, MY TIMES ARE IN YOUR HAND. SHOW ME YOUR WAYS!

August 2: Time Dynamics

Every one of us does not have access to the same amount of wealth, riches, and success, but we all have access to the same amount of TIME. We are exposed to the same dynamic operations of time which are not limited to:

1. Time usage

2. Time limitations

3. Time redemption

4. Time measurements and results

The mastery of time dynamics separates girls from women, and boys from men. We all have 24 hours, 7days, and 365days freely given to us. What we make out of it, is in proportion to our understanding of God's principles for TIME!

MEDITATION FOR THE DAY:

HOLY SPIRIT, GIVE ME AN UNDERSTANDING OF THE PRINCIPLES AND POWER OF TIME!

August 3: Time Usage

Time is one resource that can be difficult to regain when used or spent. Life is framed with so many activities that are designed to help you reach your goals or take you so far away from them.

1. To maximize the use of your time, take a critical look at the activities and events you want to get involved in.
2. Scan through them to see if these activities and events are getting you closer to your goals or taking you farther away from them.

If there is one thing that has distracted and limited us in life, I would say, it is the way we have used time to our disadvantage. "Time is the indefinite continued progress of existence and events in the past, present, and future regarded as a whole."

Please, use your time judiciously, or you will go through life with so many regrets!

MEDITATION FOR THE DAY:

HOLY SPIRIT, I RECEIVE YOUR WISDOM AND GRACE TO MAXIMIZE MY TIME!

August 4: Time Limitations

Everything that has happened, or is happening, and will happen has got limited time. Anyone engaged in the game of soccer or football knows that after a certain age, he or she can no longer be fit for competitive games. You have a limited time.

1. There is an occasion for everything and a time for every activity under heaven (Ecclesiastes 3:1 Christian Standard Bible)

Do you know the current season in your life? Are you engaging in the right activities for your life?

We all have limited time to accomplish meaningful goals and aspirations, do not let a second go without maximizing it!

MEDITATION FOR THE DAY:

HOLY SPIRIT, TEACH ME TO KNOW MY TIMES AND SEASONS IN JESUS NAME!

August 5: Time Redemption

The word redemption has many striking meanings. One is, 'that redemption is the buying back of something. Time is limited, and when not maximized, we lose the opportunities to achieve our goals and aspirations. How do you redeem lost time?

1. You can redeem a lost time by submitting your life completely to God. God alone controls time and season.
2. You can redeem the time by putting extra effort into personal development, rebuilding relationships, and having a positive outlook on life.

Jesus came to help us develop the capacity to buy back whatever we may have lost in time and life.

You can redeem lost time by believing in God and yourself and being ready to put in the work through the help of the Holy Spirit.

MEDITATION FOR THE DAY:

JESUS, THANK YOU FOR YOUR REDEMPTION, POWER, AND AT WORK IN ME!

August 6: Time Bomb

The two words – Time and Bomb, combined are defined by the Merriam-Webster dictionary as "a bomb so made as to explode at a predetermined time". Your life, like the time bomb, has its predetermined seasons to manifest YOU!

1. For the earnest expectation of the creature waiteth for the manifestation of the sons of God. (Romans 8:19 KJV)

There is so much inside of you, waiting to explode in the world. God uses time – (through challenges, pains, and obedience) to release your potential.

Your walk with Him, your diligence, and your commitment to personal development are the triggers that ignite the operations of God's 'time bomb' in your life.

MEDITATION FOR THE DAY:

HOLY SPIRIT, MANIFEST YOUR PURPOSE IN MY LIFE, IN JESUS NAME!

August 7: Time Flight

As airlines have their time of flight, time flies each day we spend on our journey living on earth. Every time we engage in activities that do not add value to us or we find ourselves in a situation that got us wondering where the time went – time flight is at work.

1. Make every moment count. Time is eternal. We are just living a portion of it on this side of eternity (earth).

We can take advantage of time flight through effective goal setting and applying ourselves to get things done through the power of the Holy Spirit. As we commune with God daily (through prayers and bible study), we receive guidance on what to invest our time and energies on.

MEDITATION FOR THE DAY:

HOLY SPIRIT, THANK YOU FOR THE WISDOM TO CEASE MOMENTS FOR YOUR GLORY!

August 8: Time Wasters

Oh, how we unconsciously allow things that seemingly look interesting, and exciting, and our past experiences, to waste the precious time God has given to us. The distractions and pressures in our lives steal and waste our valuable moments.

1. Procrastination and the blame game – putting away things that should be done and pointing the finger.
2. The distraction of today's technologies and lifestyles such as social media grip, phone meddling, television addiction, and partying spree!

Life is meaningful and purpose driven. Time tells what meaningful outcomes you will get, based on your interactions with the many time wasters staring at you daily.

Make every second count, and time will unveil the beauty of God's plan for your life.

MEDITATION FOR THE DAY: HOLY SPIRIT, KEEP ME FOCUSED ON YOUR PRIORITIES FOR MY LIFE!

August 9: Understanding Times and Seasons

One of the most amazing things that can happen to us in life, is our ability to understand the times and seasons in our lives.

1. When you have a deep knowledge of the word of God and an intimate relationship with the Holy Spirit, He uses every season and moment to fulfill His purpose in your life.

2. When you understand times and seasons, you will know what to do (the sons of Issachar knew what the nation of Israel should do – 1 Chronicles 12:32).

I desire to know each season in my life. I long to know what God will want me to do in every situation that happened, is happening, or will happen in my life.

Do you understand what is going on in your life? Do you know the season you are going through?

MEDITATION FOR THE DAY:

HOLY SPIRIT, GIVE ME A MASTERY OF TIMES AND SEASONS IN MY LIFE!

August 10: Prayer for You

Time makes up the sum of our lives. Everything we do is measured by the quality of time we put into it – relationship, career, personal development, spiritual development, and so on. I pray with you that:

God will give you mastery of times and seasons in your life.

The Holy Spirit will keep you focused on the important priorities in life.

The Spirit of God will fill you with wisdom to cease precious moments in life.

God, through the Holy Spirit will manifest His purposes in your life.

MEDITATION FOR THE DAY:

FATHER, THANK YOU FOR GRANTING ME THE GRACE TO MAXIMIZE AND BE PRODUCTIVE WITH TIME.

August 11: Times and Seasons

The words times and seasons are used to represent moments and the expression of certain things that should be happening or should happen at some point in our lives. God, in His infinite wisdom, designed certain outcomes to happen to or for you at a certain time or season.

1. Times and seasons have been designed into the number of years you are going to live on the surface of the earth.

We live in different time zones that experience different seasons such as summer, winter, spring, fall, wet, dry, sunny, hurricane, etc. So, our lives go through different seasons.

How do we recognize the seasons of our lives? How do we take advantage of these seasons? Let us find out the answers together on this timeless subject, in the next few days.

MEDITATION FOR THE DAY:

LORD JESUS, MY TIMES, AND SEASONS ARE IN YOUR HANDS!

August 12: Birth and Death

The seasons of birth and death are seasons everyone has been destined to experience. We do not have control over them, we do not choose when to be born or when to die. To make these seasons meaningful, you need to know:

1. Why were you born and what you are supposed to do?
2. What legacy you will leave behind after your death?

The things that make your life count are the activities that you get involved in between your time of birth and death. Are you purpose-driven? Do you allow the distractions of our world to drive your life? The birth and death seasons are inevitable.

What will you do with yours?

MEDITATION FOR THE DAY:

HOLY SPIRIT, HELP ME TO BE DRIVEN BY YOUR PURPOSE AS LONG AS I LIVE.

August 13: Seedtime and Harvest

One ordinance and principle, God has set to govern the existence and survival of humanity is the Seedtime and Harvest. A farmer understands that if one season is missed, the other season is doomed. God wants you to know that:

1. While the earth remains, Seedtime and harvest... Shall not cease (Genesis 8:22 NKJV).
2. Do not be fooled: You cannot cheat God. People harvest only what they plant (Galatians 6:7 NCV)

Like an IT expert will say, "Garbage in, garbage out". This season cuts across all our human endeavors – relationships, career, business, and spiritual investments. If your seed is good, your harvest will be good.

Watch what you sow in each season of your life, it will produce its double replica!

MEDITATION FOR THE DAY:

HOLY SPIRIT, HELP ME TO BE MINDFUL OF MY SEEDS!

August 14: Summer and Winter

Apart from a few states and countries in the world, most experience the seasons of winter and summer. Some people love winter more than summer, while others want year-round sunshine. Your life goes through these seasons too.

1. The winter season in your life represents times when everything looks cold and all you can do is hope and pray for God's intervention.
2. Summer represents when everything is working out as planned in your life – filled with excitement and adventures.

I wish that life can be without pains and sorrows.

However, when winter comes, remember what Jesus said, "In this godless world you will continue to experience difficulties. But take heart! I've conquered the world." (John 16:33 MSG)

MEDITATION FOR THE DAY:

IN ALL SEASONS, I AM AN OVERCOMER IN CHRIST JESUS!

August 15: Day and Night

Earth was a soup of nothingness, a bottomless emptiness, an inky blackness (Genesis 1:2 MSG). This description was a season during the creation process until God's spirit moved to recreate the chaos – darkness to light!

1. Your life has its day when your brightness, successes, trophies, and joys are celebrated and many of us pray for such seasons never to go away.
2. The night season comes with fears, uncertainties, a bleak tomorrow, and unclear paths. The best of us is formed during the night season.

The strength to go through our nights is built in the daytime.

We can never escape trials and triumphs; we must depend on the Holy Spirit to go through the days and nights of our lives.

MEDITATION FOR THE DAY: WEEPING MAY ENDURE FOR A NIGHT; MY JOY SHALL COME IN THE MORNING IN JESUS' NAME!

August 16: Season Control

Every passing season and time in our lives are ordered and controlled by laws and ordinances put in place by a non-human force. This great force ensures that each season knows its period of appearance and when it should leave the stage.

1. The seasons and times of your life are under the control of a sovereign God. He has planned out what should happen at each appointed time in your life.

Sometimes we feel our lives are running out of control and the things happening to us are beyond our control.

The secret to having a fruitful season is to continually be in step with the Holy Spirit, abide in Jesus, and be guided by the word of God.

MEDITATION FOR THE DAY:

LORD JESUS, MY TIMES, AND SEASONS ARE IN YOUR HANDS!

August 17: Seasons Change

One of the greatest quotes of all time is, "change is a constant thing" just as the seasons and times in life. Seasons change – they do not last beyond their allotted time in the schedule of nature.

1. Whatever season you are going through will change. Everything in life has got its time and season!

As human beings, we are tempted to make permanent decisions when we are going through temporary situations. I grew up hearing a popular saying, "no condition is permanent.

Seasons change, let the Holy Spirit help you through each season of your life.

MEDITATION FOR THE DAY:

FATHER, THANK YOU FOR BEING MY UNCHANGEABLE GOD!

August 18: Sense of Time

The ability to recognize the season and timing of things in one's life is of great importance. It is disastrous when a farmer is sleeping when he should be planting or complaining of hunger when he should be harvesting.

1. You must develop the inner capacity to recognize each season of your life.
2. Life will not make excuses for you, when you take for granted the demands of your seasons.

Times and seasons wait for no one. There are demands you must meet in a season that gives birth to the outcomes of another season.

Your sense of time requires that you do what is needed now, to get the results you desire in your life!

MEDITATION FOR THE DAY:

HOLY SPIRIT, GIVE ME THE ABILITY TO RECOGNIZE TIMES AND SEASONS IN MY LIFE, IN JESUS' NAME!

August 19: Beautiful Time

Times and seasons are great ordinances that determine the course of our lives. Our goals, plans, dreams, aspirations, struggles, challenges, and growth are manifested in time and season. No matter the time or season in your life:

1. God made everything beautiful in itself and in its time—but he is left us in the dark, so we can never know what God is up to, whether he's coming or going, (Ecclesiastes 3:11 MSG).

The ultimate life lesson is to yield our lives to God. "I am God, the only God you've had or ever will have—incomparable, irreplaceable—From the very beginning telling you what the ending will be." (Isaiah 46:9-10 MSG).

He (God) knows how to bring beauty out of the times and seasons in your life.

MEDITATION FOR THE DAY:

HOLY SPIRIT, THANK YOU FOR BEAUTIFYING MY TIMES AND SEASONS!

August 20: Prayer for You

In this episode of Everyday FRAGRANCE, I want to bring a reminder that our minds or brains are too small to fathom the outcomes of our lives. God alone has got our times and seasons in His hands. It is wisdom to depend on Him.

- Lord Jesus, I submit my life and future into your hands!
- Holy Spirit, my times and seasons are in your hands!
- My weeping is only for a season, my joy shall come and overcome all my sadness!
- Father, give me the ability to recognize the times and seasons in my life!
- In all seasons, I am an overcomer through Christ Jesus!

MEDITATION FOR THE DAY:

THANK YOU, HOLY SPIRIT, FOR BEAUTIFYING MY TIMES AND SEASONS.

August 21: Judgement

Today, there are great messages of transformation that encourage us, how to overcome the challenges in our lives and how to be prosperous. However, there is one message we must not forget - THE JUDGEMENT!

1. According to one of the definitions of Judgement by Webster's dictionary, "judgement is a formal utterance of an authoritative opinion".

2. For every word, action, and thought you express, there will be a formal utterance of an authoritative opinion (God has His opinion on how you are living your life).

We seem to forget that we are not destined to live for a long time on earth (the way it is now). The activity that will usher us to the next phase of our lives after the death of our physical body is judgement. "... each person is destined to die once and after that comes judgement" (Hebrew 9:27 NLT).

Are you ready to be judged?

MEDITATION FOR THE DAY:

HOLY SPIRIT, LET MY WORDS, THOUGHTS, AND ACTIONS PASS YOUR JUDGEMENT.

August 22: Self-judgement

As humans, we are quick to see what is wrong with others and most times judge them wrongly. We rarely take time to examine our words, thoughts, and actions; how they impact others, and the resulting consequences on us.

1. For if we would judge ourselves, we would not be judged. (1 Corinthians 11;13 Aramaic Bible)

To have a proper evaluation of oneself is important to self-judgement. Our world is filled with criticisms – most are not constructive; we judge people negatively without having the correct information.

Never forget that there will be a formal utterance of an authoritative opinion – judge yourself first before He does!

MEDITATION FOR THE DAY:

HOLY SPIRIT, EXAMINE MY LIFE – HELP ME TO BE MORE LIKE JESUS!

August 23: Judge Your Motive

A quick aspect of self-judgement I am writing about today is judging your motives. Our motives are "the reasons for doing something, especially one that is hidden and not obvious" (internet). Many of us have hidden motives that are selfish!

1. What are your reasons for doing the things you are doing now? What is the motive for that relationship, business, career, job, or activity?

Motives are powerful forces that drive the outcomes of every endeavor. The irony of our motives is the hidden or not obvious reasons for doing what we are doing.

If you do not judge your motive, the outcome you will get may be unfriendly.

MEDITATION FOR THE DAY:

HOLY SPIRIT, TRY MY MOTIVES AND INTENTIONS IN ALL SITUATIONS!

August 24: Judging is Tempting

How quick we are to judge others without getting the facts of the issues. This character is so natural to us, that resisting the urge is a hard thing. But is it wrong to judge others?

1. Even if it is within your reach to judge others, seek to know – ask questions.
2. Be mindful of yourself as you judge others. "Do not judge others, and you will not be judged". (Matthew 7:1 NLT)

The urge to judge others is tempting. The hurtful thing about this is, we do it to see the downfall or destruction of the other party.

Judging others wrongfully is an ungodly act. Allow others to air their position.

MEDITATION FOR THE DAY:

HOLY SPIRIT, HELP ME TO JUDGE OTHERS RIGHTLY.

August 25: On Judgement Watch

Every human activity we engage in daily is on judgement watch. Your words, your thoughts, and your actions in a relationship, business, work, and leisure will be judged. The outcome of these activities will be:

1. Judged by men, which determines what happens to you and who you become while still living on earth.

2. Judged by God – who determines your degree of success while still alive, and your place of comfort or distress in eternity after death.

We live without accountability, ignoring the consequences when alive or dead. "For your ways are in full view of the LORD, and he examines all your paths". (Proverbs 5:21 NIV).

You are on judgement watch. Live godly, every moment!

MEDITATION FOR THE DAY:

HOLY SPIRIT, GUIDE MY EVERY THOUGHT, WORD, AND ACTION!

August 26: God's Judgement

God is a just God – a good Father, Creator, and the sovereign ruler of the universe. He upholds all things by the words of His power. These words make up principles, statutes, laws, commandments, and precepts we are expected to live by.

1. When we break these rules, we activate His judgement.
2. His judgement (while we are still alive), is to correct and bring us to a renewed place of relationship with Him.

Apart from Lucifer, whose judgement was severe because of his plot of mutiny against God, God's judgement is to chastise us, not to fall into the dangers of His last day's judgement.

His (God's) judgement (chastise) while you are still alive, is to put you on the right path to enjoy eternity with Him.

MEDITATION FOR THE DAY:

HOLY SPIRIT, EXAMINE MY EVERY THOUGHT, WORD, AND ACTION!

August 27: Judgement is Real

Every day, our propensity for greed, hatred, people destruction, self-destruction (through involvement in self-destructive habits and addictions), and covetousness is alarming. We have lost our sense of self-discipline, and self-control — throwing caution to the wind.

1. Your life — your body, your soul, your spirit, and all that you have do not belong to you.
2. The one who created you will require an accounting of how you lived the life He gave you.

Why do we take God for granted and consciously choose to live our lives carelessly? His statement to the rich fool: "But God said to him, 'You fool! This very night you will have to give up your life; then who will get all these things you have kept for yourself?" — Luke 12:20 GNT.

Judgement is real, let us live responsibly!

MEDITATION FOR THE DAY: HOLY SPIRIT, LET MY LIFE BE AN EXPRESSION OF YOUR GLORY TO MY WORLD!

August 28: Antidote for Judgement

An antidote is a medicine taken or given to counteract a poison. If our lives contrast with the expectations of God, His judgement is poisonous to our lives now and after death. The antidote for this is REPENTANCE. To repent is for you to:

1. Change your inner self – your old way of thinking, and regret past sins.
2. Live your life in a way that proves repentance: seek God's purposes for your life. (Matthew 3:2 Amplified).

judgement is God's measure for humanity to stay on course, a control that assures us of our continued existence with Him after our time on earth.

Dear friends, please sincerely repent, for the kingdom of heaven is at hand!

MEDITATION FOR THE DAY:

HOLY SPIRIT, I REGRET MY PAST SINS, I CONFESS THEM AS I ACCEPT JESUS AS MY LORD AND SAVIOR.

August 29: Unplug

Every August 29 brings to my memory how precious our lives are. I can't forget when doctors asked for my consent to unplug a loved one from the ventilator. I was lost for words and heartbroken.

1. To live is a desire in every one of us, to be alive is the cry of those living on the edge of death.

2. To unplug a life or an appliance from a source should be the prerogative of the giver of that life.

The memories of our loved ones live on.

Though their lives may have been unplugged from this side of life, they are now plugged into the source of their lives.

MEDITATION FOR THE DAY:

LORD, LET MY LIFE BE FOREVER PLUGGED INTO YOU.

August 30: Prayer for You

The tides of times show the increasing reasons why judgement is inevitable. The way we treat each other and govern those God has given us the privilege to lead, and misuse our gifts, resources, and bodies is worrisome. Only genuine repentance and prayers can redeem and save us from the wrath of God's judgement.

- Holy Spirit, I regret my past sins, I confess them and accept Jesus as my Lord and Savior.
- Lord Jesus, let my life be an expression of your glory to the world!
- Holy Spirit, examine my every thought, word, and action!
- Father, help me to judge others rightly!

MEDITATION FOR THE DAY:

THANK YOU, HOLY SPIRIT, FOR MAKING ME A CANDIDATE FOR GOD'S KINGDOM.

August 31: Who are you?

As we end the leading months to the 'ember' months, I want to bring to your consciousness, the known reality of who you are. The knowledge of our self-identity is the sure foundation for our triumph in life.

1. God created you to have dominion, to reign, and to take charge of all His creation (Genesis 1:26-28)
2. God is mindful of you – He has put all things under your control (Psalm 8:4-8)

If you truly discover who you are, the issues of life will be handled differently. You were not designed to go through life alone. God still has people around, who will support you through the issues.

You are more than what you are going through!

MEDITATION FOR THE DAY:

I AM MORE THAN A CONQUEROR IN CHRIST JESUS!

September 1: Repentance

Rising every day to hear the catastrophic deaths of men, women, and children from wars, race attacks, the ravishing impact of cancerous diseases, the flex of economic and military muscles between nations, and the gross flaw in human character, the call for repentance is inevitable. To repent is to:

1. Change your inner self – your old way of thinking, and regret past sins.
2. Live your life in a way that proves repentance: seek God's purposes for your life. (Matthew 3:2 Amplified).

Friends, the times we live in are filled with uncertainties. The evils existing and living with us are real. Our only help for succor and peace in these times of chaos is to genuinely repent.

Repent (*change your inner self – your old way of thinking, regret past sins, live your life in a way that proves repentance; seek God's purpose for your life*) for the kingdom of heaven is at hand (Matthew 4:17 Amplified).

MEDITATION FOR THE DAY:

LORD JESUS, BE THE LORD OF MY LIFE!

September 2: Your Inner Self

Repentance is not just an outward expression, but the changing of the inner self – your mind or your heart. Our attraction to sin or evil starts in our hearts. Hence, the call for repentance begins with a change of your inner self.

1. Your inner self is the center of your life's transformation.
2. Your inner self is the battlefield where good and evil fight to dominate.

Your thoughts, your words, and your actions are driven by the state of your inner self. You will always produce and manifest outwardly what is inside of you. Life is "first within, then without".

Repent (*change your inner self – your old way of thinking, regret past sins, live your life in a way that proves repentance; seek God's purpose for your life*) for the kingdom of heaven is at hand (Matthew 4:17 Amplified).

MEDITATION FOR THE DAY:

LORD JESUS, CHANGE MY INNER SELF, MAKE ME MORE LIKE YOU.

September 3: Old Way of Thinking

Our repentance is dependent on how we relate to our past experiences, which impacts how we live out our thoughts. Our thoughts give birth to our acts of sins, evil, or righteousness:

1. "And no one puts new wine into old wineskins. For the wine would burst the wineskins, and the wine and the skins would both be lost. New wine calls for new wineskins". (Mark 2:22 NLT)

Our old ways of thinking are the attraction to the cares of the world through the lust of the eyes, the lust of the flesh, and the pride of life. All of these turn us against God and make us His enemies.

Repent (*change your inner self – your old way of thinking, regret past sins, live your life in a way that proves repentance; seek God's purpose for your life*) for the kingdom of heaven is at hand (Matthew 4:17 Amplified).

MEDITATION FOR THE DAY:

LORD JESUS, CHANGE MY OLD WAYS OF THINKING AND ALIGN MY THOUGHTS WITH YOUR WORD.

September 4: Regret Past Sins

True repentance takes place when the thoughts of our past sins stir a deep feeling of remorse and regret. King David demonstrated the attitude we should display when we truly regret our past sins. Please read through Psalms 51.

1. Acknowledge the past sins to God and ask for the help of the Holy Spirit to forsake them.
2. As you regret your past sins, do not let them hold you back from making progress in your relationship with God.

Our past sins can become a stronghold to our present and the future. We can be a victim and slaves of our past sins if we do not embrace the forgiveness of God. Unforsaken sins bring God's judgement.

Repent (*change your inner self – your old way of thinking, regret past sins, live your life in a way that proves repentance; seek God's purpose for your life*) for the kingdom of heaven is at hand (Matthew 4:17 Amplified).

MEDITATION FOR THE DAY:

LORD JESUS, I REPENT AND FORSAKE MY PAST SINS. I ACCEPT YOUR FORGIVENESS.

September 5: Proof of Repentance

The proof of repentance is evident in our willingness to resist, or not repeat the act of sin or evil. Repentance does not automatically sin-proof or evil-proof anyone. Sometimes, the intensity to repeat the acts surges. For your victory:

1. Stay away, as much as possible from any environments that trigger your act to sin or commit evil.
2. Consistently depend and rely on the Holy Spirit to help, guide, lead, and give you the strength to resist temptations.

It is impossible to win the battle or the struggles over sin or evil in our human flesh. The distractions and attractions to sin or commit evil are so strong. But in Christ, you can overcome always.

Repent for the kingdom of heaven is at hand.

MEDITATION FOR THE DAY:

HOLY SPIRIT, I DEPEND ON YOU. HELP ME TO RESIST THE URGE TO SIN OR COMMIT EVIL.

September 6: What's Next?

After repentance, many of us struggle with the question 'what's next? You have taken the bold step to turn back from your old ways, regretted past sins, and made up your mind to live a God-driven life. What's next?

1. At repentance, you cannot know what is next if you still want to be in control of your life. Your chances of being drawn back to sin or evil are higher.
2. The one big next thing to do is to submit to God's plans and purposes for your life.

Are you asking what those plans and purposes are? God's purpose for you is hidden inside of you. Your relationship with Him, through the study of the bible, meditation, and prayers will unlock them for you.

Repent (*change your inner self – your old way of thinking, regret past sins, live your life in a way that proves repentance; seek God's purpose for your life*) for the kingdom of heaven is at hand (Matthew 4:17 Amplified).

MEDITATION FOR THE DAY:

HOLY SPIRIT, REVEAL TO ME, YOUR PLANS AND PURPOSES FOR MY LIFE.

September 7: Dying Spiritually

God's purposes and plans for our lives are more than what the average human can comprehend. Above our cries and pursuits of mundane things, God made us take charge of the earth – rule over the earth as He rules over the heavens. But:

1. You cannot truly fulfill God's purposes in your life when your ways are not attuned to the ways of God.

2. When you disobey God's instructions, the part of you that should be connected to God begins to die – your spirit.

When we sin or enjoy acts of evil, we die spiritually. Our life's real transformation starts from our spirit. What we see with our physical eyes is the outcome of what is happening in our spirit.

Repent for the kingdom of heaven is at hand.

MEDITATION FOR THE DAY: HOLY SPIRIT, REVIVE MY SPIRIT TO BE IN ALIGNMENT WITH YOU, IN JESUS' NAME!

September 8: Signs of the Time

The call for repentance in this season cannot be overemphasized. The conflicts, disasters, catastrophes, contentions among nations of the earth, and the rise of incurable diseases happening around the world are signs to every one of us.

1. Your only assurance in these times is to anchor your soul in Jesus Christ.

The suffering in our world cannot be compared to the one after death – if our lives are not anchored in Jesus. In Jesus' words: "I have told you this so that you will have peace by being united to me. The world will make you suffer. But be brave! I have defeated the world!" (John 16:33 GNT).

Repent (*change your inner self – your old way of thinking, regret past sins, live your life in a way that proves repentance; seek God's purpose for your life*) for the kingdom of heaven is at hand (Matthew 4:17 Amplified).

MEDITATION FOR THE DAY:

HOLY SPIRIT, KEEP ME UNITED WITH JESUS IN THESE UNCERTAIN TIMES!

September 9: Salvation - Our Hope

The uncertainties, conflicts, wars, human trafficking, sexual perversion, knowledge increase, child disobedience, mass shootings, earthquakes, diseases, corruption, modern-day slavery, and many other tribulations shall not cease until the second coming of Jesus Christ.

1. How can you be saved? As the scripture says, "Everyone who calls out to the Lord for help will be saved." (Romans 10:13 GNT)

2. "Only Jesus has the power to save! His name is the only one in all the world that can save anyone." (Acts 4:12 CEV)

You and I cannot escape the dangers and catastrophe that human fallen nature has brought upon us - through sin and evil. Our only hope is in the name of Jesus Christ. *JESUS IS THE ANSWER FOR THE WORLD TODAY!*

MEDITATION FOR THE DAY:

LORD JESUS, I WILL CALL UPON YOUR NAME DAILY FOR MY SAFETY!

September 10: Prayer for You

The greatest decision and prayer anyone will ever make while still alive is the prayer of repentance and total surrender to the Lordship, and authority of Jesus Christ in his or her life. This decision and prayer influence your life now and after.

- Father, I regret my past sins, I confess them & accept Jesus as my Lord and Savior.
- Holy Spirit, revive my spirit, make me be in alignment with you!
- Father, reveal your plans and purposes for my life!
- Holy Spirit, keep me united with Jesus in these times of uncertainty!

MEDITATION FOR THE DAY:

THANK YOU, HOLY SPIRIT, FOR MAKING ME A CANDIDATE FOR GOD'S KINGDOM!

September 11: Heart State

The human heart is a strategic part of our being. It is perceived to be the center of our desires, personality, emotions, mind, intellect, will, feelings, and decisions. The human heart goes through different states at different seasons in life.

1. The state and health of your heart form your outlook on life.
2. The state and health of your heart determine your response to adversities – what you are going through and will go through.

Your heart is the storage system of your life. It receives all kinds of information from what you see and hear, to process what you think and act upon.

Your heart reveals to the world the kind of person you are. It has a state per time!

MEDITATION FOR THE DAY:

HOLY SPIRIT, I YIELD MY HEART TO YOU. MAKE MY HEART CONFORM TO YOUR WILL.

September 12: Heart Speaks

Speaking is an important part of our human daily activities. We communicate our fears, feelings, expectations, goals, and dreams when we voice them out, through our mouths. Your mouth is what gives your heart a voice.

1. Your heart is the starting process of the things you utter.
2. The words, phrases, figures of speech, and numbers that you drop during conversation come from the 'abundance' in your heart.

Your heart is the center drive of your speech center. Your heart speaks what you have inside through its co-partner: Your mouth.

Every time you speak, you are speaking out your heart, and your heart is a critical part of your being. Guard it!

MEDITATION FOR THE DAY:

HOLY SPIRIT, I YIELD MY HEART TO YOU. GUARD IT!

September 13: Heart Control

Every written material, product, and content in our human spheres has one strategic goal: 'to control our hearts and our decisions. TV programs, social media content, and the happenings in our environment control you.

1. Whatever or whomever you permit to control your heart, automatically controls your life.

God created us to execute His will through us on earth. The devil influences our hearts to also execute his purposes.

The media and other influencing factors in our environment seek to control our hearts to achieve a goal. Guard your heart!

MEDITATION FOR THE DAY:

HOLY SPIRIT, I YIELD THE CONTROL OF MY HEART TO YOU.

September 14: Heart Abundance

We live in a world where the resources in the air, on land, and in the sea are enough to meet the basic needs of the infinite number of people residing in it. Yet, the wealth of 97% of the population of the world is in the hands of the remaining 3%.

1. The abundance of your heart is driven by what you feed it.
2. The greatest source of your heart's abundance is the word of God – The Bible.

Your heart gives your eyes its worldview (how you see and perceive things). Whatever is in your heart, creates the state of wealth, poverty, sickness, problems, opportunities, successes, growth, good, and evil in your life.

Guard your heart!

MEDITATION FOR THE DAY:

HOLY SPIRIT, FILL MY HEART WITH THE ABUNDANCE OF YOUR WORDS!

September 15: Heart Treasury

The world's treasuries are stored up in secret vaults, secret undergrounds, banks, and other financial institutions, to meet the economic needs of nations and individuals. Your heart stores the treasury you need to live a life of success or failure.

1. All your experiences, training, learning, growth, development, and interactions with your environment, are treasures being stored up.

The treasures you have stored up over time, begin to form the real you. The real you manifest through the overflow of your heart.

"A good person produces good things from the treasury of a good heart, and an evil person produces evil things from the treasury of an evil heart" (Luke 6:45 NLT). Guard your heart!

MEDITATION FOR THE DAY:

HOLY SPIRIT, FILL MY HEART WITH THE TREASURES OF HEAVEN.

September 16: Evil Heart

The heart has a dynamic working built into it, that gives it the ability to retain good and evil. But with the stronghold of sin-nature, the presence of evil in our hearts seems to have overridden the good we can show.

1. As from the abundance of a good heart, good things are spoken, so also from the abundance of an evil heart, evil words and actions are manifested.

The nature of good or evil comes from the sources of information that you allow into your heart. What goes into your heart is what either make you good or evil. "...and an evil person produces evil things from the treasury of an evil heart" (Luke 6:45 NLT).

Guard your heart!

MEDITATION FOR THE DAY:

HOLY SPIRIT, I YIELD MY HEART TO YOU. OVERSHADOW ME WITH YOUR GOODNESS.

September 17: Fool's Heart

God created and gave us a heart that is designed to function according to His views, perspectives, and principles. But the intake of what we allow into our hearts, and what we say from the abundance of what is deposited in it, is at our will.

1. Only fools say in their hearts, "There is no God." (Psalm 14:1)

The will (the ability to make our choices), has made us independent of God who gave us will-power. The story of the rich fool in the bible (Luke 12: 13-21) should serve as a reminder to us – "But God said to him, 'You fool! You will die this very night. Then who will get everything you worked for?'

Honor God, guard your heart!

MEDITATION FOR THE DAY:

MY FATHER, MY GOD, I BELIEVE IN YOUR EXISTENCE, I YIELD MY HEART TO YOU, IN JESUS' NAME.

September 18: Merry Heart

The troubles, worries, and concerns in living in this beautiful world of ours, can be overwhelming. The worries of how to survive, and succeed in a career, business, family, and relationships can be overarching. The burden of all of these breaks our bodies, soul, and spirit. But:

1. A merry heart is a good medicine: but a broken spirit drieth up the bones. (Proverbs 17:22 ERV)

Our human tendencies and flaws will always bring sadness and restlessness to our hearts. The way out is to keep our heart on God, who alone gives the kind of peace that brings a merry heart.

"You will keep in perfect peace all who trust in you, all whose thoughts are fixed on you!" (Isaiah 26:3 NLT). Guard your heart!

MEDITATION FOR THE DAY:

HOLY SPIRIT, I FIX MY THOUGHTS ON YOU, I RECEIVE A MERRY HEART IN THE MIDST OF LIFE'S STORMS!

September 19: Prayer for You

The seat of our life's decisions is the heart. The decisions we make, or take are from the amount of information we have stored over time. "Above all else, guard your heart, for everything you do flows from it." (Proverbs 4:23 NIV)

- Holy Spirit, I yield the control of my heart to you.
- Holy Spirit, I give my heart to you, for the fullness of your words.
- Holy Spirit, revive my heart from every brokenness and sinful thought.
- Holy Spirit, fill my heart with your love and grace.
- Holy Spirit, fill my heart with joy and laughter.

MEDITATION FOR THE DAY:

THANK YOU, HOLY SPIRIT, FOR MAKING ME A CANDIDATE FOR GOD'S KINGDOM.

September 20: Making Choices 1

One of the amazing opportunities and power that was given to man at creation is the ability to make choices. "Choice is defined as an act of selecting or making a decision when faced with two or more possibilities". (Google search).

1. The choice you make between two or among many possibilities determines the positive or negative results you get in your life.

Our desire to choose is God's. Your being alive was His choice – "Even before he made the world, God loved us and chose us in Christ…" (Ephesians 1:4 NLT).

God is mindful of the choices we make in our lives. Your present position or circumstances today is a result of the choice or decision you made.

Choose Right!

MEDITATION FOR THE DAY:

HOLY SPIRIT, HELP ME TO MAKE CHOICES IN ALIGNMENT WITH GOD'S PLANS.

September 21: Making Choices 2

There is so much going on in our lives today. The noise, distractions, pursuits, pressures, needs, wants, relationships, media, politics, family, pains, pleasures, and so much more are constantly compelling you and me to make a choice.

1. The choice you make defines who you are and what you will become – it shows where your heart's allegiance is.

The choices we make define our priorities. These choices are driven by the need to confirm the supremacy of two operating forces on earth – good or evil, light or darkness. How then, do we know the right choice to make?

Choose Right!

MEDITATION FOR THE DAY:

HOLY SPIRIT, GIVE ME THE WISDOM TO MAKE THE RIGHT CHOICES IN LIFE.

September 22: Decision Determine Destiny

One of my mentors and ministry shaper always uses the statement that "your decision determines your destiny", each time he is making an altar call, or buttressing a point for you to be strategic when making decisions.

Every decision you make or take determines an outcome in your life. "If you are willing and obedient, you will eat the best from the land. (Isaiah 1:19 GNT). We always have a choice to make.

Your destiny, whether it is adventurous, exciting, boring, or filled with regrets, is a result of the decision or choices you made.

Your career, your relationship, business, location, and ministry are all playing out because you made a choice.

Choose Right!

MEDITATION FOR THE DAY:

HOLY SPIRIT, YOU KNOW MY DESTINY, HELP ME MAKE THE RIGHT CHOICES ALWAYS!

September 23: Product of Choice

Science tells us that an average of 100million sperm is released during sexual intercourse, and only one is needed to start the conception of a baby in the womb. No man or woman knows how the selection process is made, but God – who gives life.

1. "I knew you before I formed you in your mother's womb. (Jeremiah 1:5 NLT)

Everyone alive or who ever lived on earth is a product of God's choice. And I know, God chose right by making you the one that was conceived.

Your life's choices are in the wisdom of God's plans for you.

Choose Right!

MEDITATION FOR THE DAY:

FATHER, THANK YOU FOR CHOOSING ME!

September 24: Choice Made Easy

It is worrisome to know how many times many of us fail repeatedly or get into trouble with the choices we make despite the better alternative. I am chief of all, who falter at this. In you lies the ability to make the right choice.

1. "Now listen! Today I am giving you a choice between life and death, between prosperity and disaster. (Deuteronomy 30:15 NLT)

The options before us daily have the potential to bring life and death or prosperity and disaster to us. Whether it is a relationship, financial, spiritual, career, or business decision – they will bring you life, death, prosperity, or disaster.

Choose Right!

MEDITATION FOR THE DAY:

HOLY SPIRIT, I DEPEND ON YOU TO MAKE THE BEST CHOICES IN LIFE.

September 25: Wisdom in Choice

Oh! how we struggle and strive to make the best or right choices in our lives. Our human nature and quest to gratify our flesh make it difficult to make the right choice in the glaring face of the consequences. There is a pearl of available wisdom on how to make the right choice.

1. Look at what I have done for you today... Love God, your God. Walk in his ways. Keep his commandments, regulations, and rules so that you will live, really live, live exuberantly, blessed by God, your God, in the land you are about to enter and possess" Deuteronomy 30:15-16 MSG).

The wisdom to make the right choices is in obedience and alignment with God's rules of engagement. Every decision you and I must make has its governing regulations given to us by our heavenly father and creator.

Obey what God says and you will always Choose Right!

MEDITATION FOR THE DAY: HOLY SPIRIT, HELP ME LIVE BY THE REGULATIONS OF GOD IN MAKING LIFE'S CHOICES.

September 26: Choosing is Hard

The decision and process of making a choice between two, or among so many possibilities can be hard! Is it about choosing a spouse? Is it about a career path? Business? Relocation? Relationships? The list is unending. How can we make the right choice?

1. Do not always be in a hurry. Many of us make unnecessary mistakes or wrong choices because we hurriedly decide.
2. Trust absolutely in God to guide you in the process. God's choice for you has a far better end.

"Therefore, thus says the Lord GOD: "Behold, I lay in Zion a stone for a foundation, A tried stone, a precious cornerstone, a sure foundation; Whoever believes will not act hastily." (Isaiah 28:16).

With God, you will always make the best choice.

MEDITATION FOR THE DAY:

HOLY SPIRIT, TEACH ME TO WAIT AND TRUST IN YOU, FOR THE BEST CHOICE.

September 27: Choice Have Witnesses

Every time we are faced with a decision to make concerning our relationships, career, business, destiny, or ministry; there are seen and unseen witnesses watching to see how those choices are made.

1. "Right now, I call the sky and the earth to be witnesses that I am offering you this choice. Will you choose for the Lord to make you prosperous and give you a long life? Or will he put you under a curse and kill you? Choose life!" (Deuteronomy 30:19 CEV).

There are laws governing the operations of the seen and unseen world, set in motion when you make a choice. It is wise to allow God's regulations and purposes, to be the determinant of all your choices in life.

Choose Right!

MEDITATION FOR THE DAY:

HOLY SPIRIT, HELP ME LIVE BY THE REGULATIONS OF GOD IN MAKING LIFE'S CHOICES.

September 28: Redeem Wrong Choices

My choices in life have taken me to this point. The right choices that I made can be counted, but my wrong choices are so many. The consequences, regrets, disappointments, and shame that came from most of them, hurt! But thank God for His redemption:

1. "I didn't come to invite good people to turn to God. I came to invite sinners." (Luke 5:32).

Making the right choices in life is not based on righteousness. Neither is our making the wrong choice based on our sinfulness. Jesus came to redeem us from our past wrongs and to request our dependence on Him. "Come to me, all you who are weary and burdened, and I will give you rest". (Matthew 11:28 NET Bible). He wants to redeem you now; let Him help you.

Above all, let Him (God) influence your choices.

MEDITATION FOR THE DAY: FATHER, I KNOW I HAVE MADE SOME WRONG CHOICES IN MY LIFE; LET THE REDEMPTIVE POWER OF JESUS GRANT ME RESTORATION AGAIN.

September 29: Prayer for You

Decisions, decisions, and decisions! Choices, choices, and choices! These two words make men and women. These words are the reflection of the seen world. Your choices and decisions produce the quality of your life. Let us pray & declare:

- Holy Spirit, save me from wrong decisions and choices.
- Holy Spirit, heal and restore me from my wrong decisions and choices in the past.
- Holy Spirit, teach me to trust and wait on you in the process of making choices.

MEDITATION FOR THE DAY:

HOLY SPIRIT, BE THE GREATEST INFLUENCE IN MY DECISIONS AND CHOICES.

September 30: You and Your-Self

The beauty and wonders of God's creation are incomplete without the presence of God's masterpiece – YOU! The making of you – your form, your looks, your potential, your abilities, and so much more, can only have been for yourself and a reason.

1. "You formed my innermost being, shaping my delicate   inside and my intricate outside, and wove them all together in my mother's womb". (Psalms 139:13 TPT).

However, the sum of what makes you who you are may never be seen or known, if you do not put to work what God has deposited in you. In some ways, many of us have given up on life because of the pressures, worries, and challenges that we have or are going through.

God created you for a purpose – LIVE FOR IT!

MEDITATION FOR THE DAY:

MY FATHER, GOD, AND CREATOR, I WANT TO LIVE FOR WHAT YOU CREATED ME TO BE.

October 1: Self-Discovery

Happy new month! The year is gradually closing its door in readiness to go off the stage of time and season. So much has been discovered in the different frontiers of our world – politics, economy, etc. But did you discover or rediscover anything about yourself?

1. "Self-discovery is the act or process of achieving self-knowledge" – Merriam Webster

Over 96% of the world's population is living below their potential because we struggle with our identity. Self-discovery starts from knowing whose you are, and who you are. "It is through him that we live and function and have our identity…" (Acts 17:28 TPT).

If you discover God, you will discover yourself! LIVE FOR IT!

MEDITATION FOR THE DAY:

HOLY SPIRIT, HELP TO SEE ME, THE WAY, YOU SEE ME!

October 2: Self-Development

The goal of self-discovery is to help us identify the abilities, gifts, talents, and graces that God has given to us. All of these will remain as potential until we apply ourselves to harnessing, developing, sharpening, and putting them to daily use.

1. "If the axe is dull and its edge unsharpened, more strength is needed, but skill will bring success". (Ecclesiastes 10:10 NIV)

Self-development is the process through which you sharpen your skill in the areas of your strengths, gifts, talents, and abilities. There is nothing that can stop your success in life, if you give attention to studying, learning, training, mentorship, cultivating the act of getting things done, and following the lead of the Holy Spirit!

GIVE ATTENTION TO IT (*Self-development*)!

MEDITATION FOR THE DAY:

HOLY SPIRIT, I RECEIVE YOUR GRACE FOR PERSONAL DEVELOPMENT!

October 3: Self-Mastery

One of the benefits that we can get from self-development is self-mastery. With self-mastery, you become irresistible, a magnet that no quality metal can resist. Self-mastery is what separates boys from men, and girls from women.

1. "Show me someone who does a good job, and I will show you someone who is better than most and worthy of the company of kings". (Proverbs 22:29 GNT)

The mastery of the self brings maturity, contentment, and poise. The world is looking for people who have mastered their emotions, have a good sense of judgement, and command the respect of others. Do not take yourself for granted, strive for self-mastery always!

Strive for mastery in all you do!

MEDITATION FOR THE DAY:

HOLY SPIRIT, HELP ME TO MASTER MYSELF, THROUGH YOUR INFLUENCE!

October 4: Self-Discipline

Self-discipline is one area of human grace that many of us struggle with every day. The goal of self-mastery cannot be achieved without self-discipline. Self-discipline helps us master our emotions, control our appetites, delay gratification, and Self-leadership

1. "I discipline my body like an athlete, training it to do what it should. Otherwise, I fear that after preaching to others I myself might be disqualified." (1 Corinthians 9:27 NLT)

To achieve meaningful goals in our lives, we must train our minds, spirit, soul, and body to resist distractions, weaknesses, and peer pressures from our environment.

Self-actualization comes with a price – it is called DISCIPLINE! LIVE FOR IT!

MEDITATION FOR THE DAY:

HOLY SPIRIT, HELP ME TO SUBJECT MYSELF TO YOUR DISCIPLINE!

October 5: Selfie

The advent of smartphones gave rise to an innovative way that enables us to take pictures of ourselves, with friends, family, and even strangers. The image that is reproduced reflects our different postures– standings, facial expressions, gestures, etc.

1. Do you take time to capture a selfie of your life – where you have been, where you are, and where you want to go?
2. When you do, what do you see?

The need for self-examination is important for our life-long success. Many of us would rather give our energy to criticizing others than taking a personal selfie. "Examine me, O LORD, and test me! Evaluate my inner thoughts and motives!" (Psalm 26:2 NET Bible)! LIVE FOR IT!

MEDITATION FOR THE DAY:

HOLY SPIRIT, EXAMINE ME, AND EVALUATE MY INNER THOUGHTS AND MOTIVES!

October 6: Selfish

For many of us that believe in the creation story and have read about Eve's encounter with the serpent, you will agree with me on the definition of the word 'selfish'. And if you look closely – you will see the cause of humanity's problems:

1. Selfish means to be "concerned excessively or exclusively with oneself: seeking or concentrating on one's own advantage, pleasure, or well-being without regard for others". Merriam-Webster Dictionary.

It is not wrong to seek good things or privileges for oneself, but when it is to the disadvantage of others, then it is selfishness. If we think about others, most of our actions will be properly guided.

"Whenever people are jealous or selfish, they cause trouble and do all sorts of cruel things.!" (James 3:16 CEV)! LIVE FOR IT!

MEDITATION FOR THE DAY:

HOLY SPIRIT, HELP ME TO BE SENSITIVE IN MY DEALINGS WITH OTHERS IN JESUS' NAME!

October 7: Self-Esteem

There is a great statement that has propelled me to be the best of me, as much as I can, "the largest room in the world, is the room for improvement". To give yourself continuous self-improvement, you need to have healthy self-esteem of yourself.

1. "Self-esteem means to have confidence in one's worth or abilities; self-respect." – Google.

Many of us struggle with the challenge of low self-esteem. The temptation to beat down on ourselves comes after failures, disappointments, rejections, or when we do not have or feel others are better than us.

No! You are special: "I will praise You because I have been remarkably and wonderfully made" (Psalms 139:14 HCSB)

MEDITATION FOR THE DAY:

HOLY SPIRIT, MY SELF-ESTEEM IS IN KNOWING, THAT I AM MADE IN GOD'S IMAGE!

October 8: Self-Fulfilment

Welling up inside every one of us is the desire to reach the peak of our potential and achievement in life. lying subtly behind our daily pursuits to grow in our career, build a profitable business, acquire degrees and certifications, and gain the respect of others, is the genuine desire to achieve our hopes and dreams.

1. "Self-Fulfilment is a feeling of satisfaction that you have achieved what you wanted". Cambridge Dictionary.

There is nothing like looking back, seeing how far you have come, and the spirit of joy surging through your body. "I've run hard right to the finish, believed all the way. All that's left now is the shouting—God's applause!" (2 Timothy 4:7 MSG).

Your self-fulfillment is in God's purpose and design for your life. LIVE FOR IT!

MEDITATION FOR THE DAY:

HOLY SPIRIT, MY SELF-FULFILMENT IS IN YOU – MY PURPOSE AND ASSIGNMENT ON EARTH.

October 9: Self-Destruct

In our quest to experience the height of self-actualization, many of us have thrown caution to the wind. What we never imagined could be the outcome of our lives, has become our daily battles because of addictions – sex, drugs, greed, short temper, and lack of self-control. We feel helpless and struggle with our actions.

1. "For I do not understand my own actions. For I do not do what I want, but I do the very thing I hate". (Romans 7:15 ESV)

Every action we take that lines up with the works of the flesh (Galatians 5:19-21) leads to self-destruction.

There's hope!

"Yield freely and fully to (Jesus Christ), the dynamic life and power of the Holy Spirit, you will abandon the cravings of yourself - life, (Galatians 5:16 TPT)! LIVE FOR IT!

MEDITATION FOR THE DAY:

HOLY SPIRIT, I YIELD MY LIFE TO YOU, DELIVER ME FROM SELF-DESTRUCTIVE CRAVINGS!

October 10: Prayer for you

The act of self-transformation and self-improvement can be an uphill task. But the rewards and self-confidence that come from applying yourself to practices, principles, orders, boundaries, and systems are worth the process. Let us pray:

- Father, help me to see me, the way you see.
- Forgive my limitations of myself and help me yield the whole of me to you.
- Holy Spirit, deliver me from self-destructive cravings and habits.
- Holy Spirit, heal and restore me from addictions and emotional tantrums.

MEDITATION FOR THE DAY:

HOLY SPIRIT, HELP ME TO REACH THE HEIGHT OF MY LIFE'S FULFILMENT.

October 11: Spiritual Disciplines

Life is governed by rules, systems, conduct, and activities that shape your future and daily pursuits. Our capacity to align with these rules, systems, conducts, and activities is "discipline". And the chief of all disciplines are the spiritual ones:

1. "Physical exercise has some value, but spiritual exercise is valuable in every way, because it promises life both for the present and for the future." (1 Timothy 4:8 GNT)

There are forces unseen that control our spaces and lives that education, expertise, beauty, and wealth cannot withstand for too long.

Many of us pay much attention to mental, physical, emotional, and financial disciplines to the detriment of spiritual disciplines – that guarantee sustainability, for "the now and the future."

MEDITATION FOR THE DAY:

HOLY SPIRIT, HELP ME TO BE DISCIPLINED IN MY SPIRITUAL LIFE, IN JESUS' NAME!

October 12: Worship - Ministering to God

The top of all spiritual disciplines is the act of worship! Every spiritual authority or being seeks the worship of you and me - God, Satan, and even man. Who you worship determines the sustainability of your wealth, health, and even your life after death.

1. "Jesus answered him, "Get behind me Satan! For it is written, 'You shall worship the Lord your God, and you shall serve him only.'"." (Luke 4:8 World English Bible)

Worship is to honor or show reverence for a divine being or supernatural power. God wants you to worship or minister to Him with your life, your time, your wealth, your career, your job, your business, and your future.

Worship Him ONLY!

MEDITATION FOR THE DAY:

WORSHIP THE LORD, O MY SOUL AND ALL THAT IS WITHIN ME, IN JESUS' NAME!

October 13: Prayer and Fasting

Two spiritual disciplines that have been known to be the most difficult ones for many Christians are prayer and fasting. Surprisingly, these disciplines are the anchor to others and the ones that disrupt the challenges we face in any area of our lives.

1. "Howbeit this lineage of demons does not go out but by prayer and fasting." (Matthew 17:21 Jubilee Bible 2000)

There is a lineage of demons behind the problems many of us are encountering today. To overcome them, we must engage the power of God in prayers and fasting. Do not let the devil override you with your excuses, and assumptions that you cannot fast or pray.

Take charge of your spiritual life now!

MEDITATION FOR THE DAY:

HOLY SPIRIT, I RECEIVE THE SPIRIT OF GRACE AND SUPPLICATION IN THE NAME OF JESUS!

October 14: Word In-Take

It has been proven age-longed, that words shape our lives. The world and everything that is in it was created by the power of words – "and God said"! A core spiritual discipline is developing the habit of studying the bible:

1. "For the word of God is alive and powerful. It is sharper than the sharpest two-edged sword, cutting between soul and spirit, between joint and marrow. It exposes our innermost thoughts and desires." (Hebrews 4:12 NLT)

The chaos and uncertainties in our world today were created by our words and actions. The only remedy to it will be a higher level of spoken words acted out.

God's word (the Bible) transforms in any situation if cultivated as a habit or discipline.

MEDITATION FOR THE DAY:

HOLY SPIRIT, LET THE WORD OF GOD DWELL IN ME RICHLY, IN THE NAME OF JESUS!

October 15: Meditation Activates

One infinite spiritual discipline, that many of the religions in the world practice with great results, is meditation. Meditation activates your faith in your expectations. It brings the unseen to reality and makes your imagination break the limits of impossibilities. What you meditate on also matters.

1. "Study this Book of Instruction continually. Meditate on it day and night so you will be sure to obey everything written in it. Only then will you prosper and succeed in all you do." (Joshua 1:8 NLT)

The results we see in our lives are the outcomes of our prevailing meditations (what we think about). What you think about, you bring about.

Let God's word be what you think concerning any issue in your life. It is sealed with "THE BLOOD".

MEDITATION FOR THE DAY:

HOLY SPIRIT, LET MY HEART, EYES, AND EARS, BE FIXED ON THE WORD OF GOD!

October 16: Share your Story

Every day, the pain and frustration people go through in their lives are unimaginable. The joy of living, or the possibility of a better tomorrow, is a mere dream or hope for many. Sharing your story of God's help is one discipline that our world needs.

1. "How can people have faith in the Lord and ask him to save them, if they have never heard about him? And how can they hear, unless someone tells them?" (Romans 10:14 CEV)

The spiritual discipline of sharing your story (faith), helps you grow in your walk with God. Also, it boosts the strength, comfort, and hope others need to go on when they hear the testimonies of God's mercies and favor to you.

Share your story today, it will help one-person face and overcome the challenges in their lives.

MEDITATION FOR THE DAY:

HOLY SPIRIT, USE MY LIFE TO STRENGTHEN AND ENCOURAGE ONE PERSON, EACH DAY.

October 17: Nothing is Yours

The need to acquire the best things in life, provide for our loved ones, and to survive drives our pursuit of wealth and success. All of these are vital for our living, but we must not forget that we are stewards of all that we have or achieve.

1. "A person cannot receive even one thing unless God bestows it." (John 3:27 TPT)
2. "...it is required [as essential and demanded] of stewards that one be found faithful and trustworthy". (1 Corinthians 4:2 AMP)

Stewardship – being accountable for the blessings of God in your life, is a spiritual disciple you must cultivate. Nothing that we have is ours – they were given to us temporarily.

Be a great steward. God will ask you on judgement day!

MEDITATION FOR THE DAY:

HOLY SPIRIT, HELP ME TO BE A GREAT STEWARD OF ALL THAT YOU HAVE GIVEN TO ME!

October 18: Secret to Abundance

The degree of attacks against the discipline of giving to the church or for the advancement of God's kingdom purposes on earth is unimaginable! As much as the shortcomings of leaders in the areas of governance, accountability, and transparency are worrisome, the spiritual discipline of giving is for you and not for others.

1. "Give, and you will receive. Your gift will return to you in full pressed down, shaken together to make room for more, running over, and poured into your lap. The amount you give will determine the amount you get back." (Luke 6:38 NLT)

The law of sowing and reaping can never be broken, even with the weaknesses of men or women. Your giving to God is a secret weapon of preservation and provision for you and your family.

Increase in your giving; you will experience an abundance.

MEDITATION FOR THE DAY:

HOLY SPIRIT, I RECEIVE THE GRACE TO GIVE BEYOND MEASURE IN JESUS' NAME!

October 19: Exercise your Authority

The spiritual discipline of enforcing our authority has been ignored by many. At creation, God gave us a mandate to take charge of our environment and the circumstances around us. The reverse is the case, life and circumstances are harassing us daily.

1. "Jesus called his twelve disciples and gave them authority to force evil spirits out of people and to cure every disease and sickness." (Matthew 10:1 GNT)

We have been given the authority to enforce the plans of God concerning our lives. We cannot overcome the forces that control our lives if our spiritual lives lack the influence of the Holy Spirit.

You must cultivate these few spiritual disciplines, to surmount the harassment of the devil in your life.

MEDITATION FOR THE DAY:

HOLY SPIRIT, I RECEIVE YOUR POWER AND AUTHORITY TO OVERCOME IN LIFE!

October 20: Prayer for You

Growing in spiritual disciplines is inevitable for every child of God. "Be on your guard and stay awake. Your enemy, the devil, is like a roaring lion, sneaking around to find someone to attack". (1 Peter 5:8 CEV). Let us pray:

- Father, thank you for the grace to keep growing spiritually.
- Holy Spirit, pour into my life your spirit of grace and supplication.
- Holy Spirit, increase my hunger and thirst for your word.
- Holy Spirit, let my life be your testimony to the saved and unsaved.

MEDITATION FOR THE DAY:

HOLY SPIRIT, EMPOWER ME TO DO EXPLOITS IN LIFE!

October 21: Character Formation

Psychologists and Philosophers coined the term "Tabula Rasa" (blank slate), meaning every human was born with a blank state of mind. Our traits, behaviors, actions, and character are formed because of our experiences, knowledge, and perceptions.

1. "Character is one of the attributes or features that make up and distinguish an individual." (Merriam Webster dictionary)

"Just as water reflects the face, so the heart reflects the person". (Proverbs 27:19 ISV). Character is formed in your heart as you cultivate godly virtues which we will explore in this series.

Our world needs men and women with great character!

MEDITATION FOR THE DAY:

HOLY SPIRIT, HELP ME CULTIVATE VIRTUES THAT REFLECT THE CHARACTER OF GOD.

October 22: The Character of Love

Character formation is the sum of many virtues that we have cultivated over time. These virtues are not ordinarily the products of our abilities or our making, but by the operation of God's spirit working through and in us. These virtues that aid character formation is called the fruit of the spirit:

1. "But the fruit of the Spirit [the result of His presence within us] is love [unselfish concern for others], joy, [inner] peace, patience [not the ability to wait, but how we act while waiting], kindness, goodness, faithfulness, gentleness, self-control. Against such things there is no law." (Galatians 5:22-23 AMP)

The character of love is manifested in the face of hatred, human shortcomings, and the glaring possibilities of unforgiveness. It takes our consciousness of God's presence in us to love others.

Love governs our human relationship – grow in it!

MEDITATION FOR THE DAY:

HOLY SPIRIT, HELP ME TO CULTIVATE THE CHARACTER OF LOVE.

October 23: Joy in You

One character that we all struggle to develop is how to be 'Joy-full'. How can we cultivate the act of being filled with joy when everything around us is falling apart? The hurts, disappointments, and even the bad news we hear every day drain joy out of us.

1. The character of being joyful is not developed when all things are going well for you. Joy is developed when nothing is working

2. "Consider it nothing but joy, my brothers and sisters, whenever you fall into various trials". (James 1:2 AMP)

It is humanly absurd to be joyful when the trials of life are drowning you. Your joy will never come from what is happening outside but from the state of your inside.

Your relationship with God is the secret of being joyful. "Don't be dejected and sad, for the joy of the Lord is your strength!" (Nehemiah 8:10 NLT).

MEDITATION FOR THE DAY:

HOLY SPIRIT, FILL ME WITH YOUR JOY THAT COMES FROM WITHIN, IN JESUS' NAME!

October 24: Peace in Chaos

After the disobedience of the first man and woman, the distress and restlessness that greets us day in and day out is heavy. We live in a world where each day comes with its fears, troubles, noise, and struggles. Peace has eluded the average person.

1. "You will keep him in perfect peace, whose mind is stayed on You, because he trusts in You." (Isaiah 26:3 MEV)

Finding inner peace in our restless and troubling world is a tall order. Cultivating the character of being peaceful is possible as you trust in God. "…Here on earth, you will have many trials and sorrows; but cheer up, for I have overcome the world." (John 16:33 TLB).

What are joy and excitement that Jesus Christ brought peace to us! Turn to Him.

MEDITATION FOR THE DAY:

HOLY SPIRIT, I RECEIVE YOUR PEACE IN THE TRIALS AND SORROWS OF LIFE!

October 25: Searching for Patience

Thinking about the word "Patience' alone, can make the average human belly cringe. We are on the fast lane to achieving more, and we lose sight of what matters. The character of being 'Patient" is a scarce commodity in our world today.

1. "By your patient endurance, you will gain your souls." (Luke 21:19 BLB)

Our human differences and tendencies make it hard to be patient with ourselves and with others. This weakness has spilled over to our relationship with God. "Patience is not the ability to wait, but how we act while waiting".

Patience gives you mastery over situations and gives you fresh perspectives into the circumstances!

MEDITATION FOR THE DAY:

HOLY SPIRIT, I RECEIVE YOUR SPIRIT OF ENDURANCE IN ALL LIFE'S SITUATIONS!

October 26: Be Kind-Full

Kindness is one attribute every one of us can do, to spice up our lives. The brashness of our human nature, the reality of the harsh economic situation, and the fear of the unknown make this soothing character difficult to come by.

1. "And be kind to one another, tender-hearted, forgiving each other, as also in Christ God forgave you." (Ephesians 4:32 Berean Literal Bible)

Kindness does not mean a thing when you are at peace with others. The act of kindness is activated when others hurt your feelings, and your heart is still tender for God to heal, deal with the situations, and provide a covering over you. Kindness attracts God's forgiveness.

Do not wish others evil. Be Kind-full as God is to you!

MEDITATION FOR THE DAY:

HOLY SPIRIT, HELP ME TO BE KIND TO THOSE THAT HURT ME. WRAP ME IN YOUR ARMS.

October 27: Being Good

Someone special said to me that anyone can be good! I took some time to brood about this. Is it possible for anyone to be good with the evil around us, the deception of humanity, and the increase in self-centeredness?

1. Being a good person is not automatic because you are a Christian. Your goodness is influenced by your experience, environment, and upbringing

2. The nature of goodness is enhanced as you cultivate the nature of Christ

It can be difficult to be good to others especially when you have experienced disappointments and hurt people. The uniqueness of good people is their desire to let God's nature flow through them.

"You however are to be complete in goodness, as your Heavenly Father is complete." (Matthew 5:48 Weymouth NT).

MEDITATION FOR THE DAY:

FATHER, YOUR GOODNESS FLOWS THROUGH ME DAILY.

October 28: Faithful to Who?

One character in demand today is FAITHFULNESS! God wants it from us, and our fellow human beings want it from us. We all seek someone who will be committed and faithful to us for all seasons of our lives – in good or bad times.

1. Expecting faithfulness or loyalty from others because of what we do or have done for them may be faulty (we are not perfect people!)

2. God expresses His faithfulness to us not by what we have done or did not do. "If we are faithless, he remains faithful— for he cannot deny himself." (2 Timothy 2:13 ESV)

Faithfulness is costly – you will be hurt, disappointed, and even abandoned. It could be in marriage, spiritual, business, or any human activities (we hurt each other somehow).

Your safety net is in God – His healing, peace, and perspectives are birthed in your heart as you make Him your sole focus of FAITHFULNESS!

MEDITATION FOR THE DAY: HOLY SPIRIT, HELP ME TO BE FAITHFUL TO YOU AND THOSE YOU HAVE PUT IN MY PATH.

October 29: Are you Gentle?

Gentleness is having a character of kindness, tenderness, and being calm. It is increasingly difficult to find this trait in many of us. We live in a world where swiftness, aggression, brashness, and impatience govern daily.

1. Those who tend to be calm and easy-going are looked on as weak, not smart enough, and not strong.
2. Those with gentle and calm spirits bring unusual peace and tranquility to situations and human relationships.

We can see what smartness, hardness of heart, and insensitivity are bringing up our world today. "God loves you and has chosen you as his own special people. So be gentle…" (Colossians 3:12 CEV).

Strength and wisdom are displayed in calmness

MEDITATION FOR THE DAY:

HOLY SPIRIT, CLOTHE ME WITH THE GARMENT OF MEEKNESS IN JESUS' NAME!

October 30: Control Yourself

Self-Control! Self-Control!! Self-Control!!! Lord, help us. Our lives may not have great meaning if we cannot discipline ourselves to overcome the desires and passions that seek to control us. Self-control starts from your spirit (heart):

1. He that hath no rule over his own spirit is like a city that is broken down, and without walls (Proverbs 25:28 KJV)
2. Losing self-control leaves you as helpless as a city without a wall.

Our lack of self-control gets us into trouble. The rage of anger, sexual seduction, greed, corruption, and uncontrolled appetites leave us open to demonic influences.

To develop the character of self-control, "let the Lord Jesus Christ be as near to you as the clothes you wear. Then you won't try to satisfy your selfish desires." (Romans 13:14 CEV)

MEDITATION FOR THE DAY:

HOLY SPIRIT, LET MY HEART BE FILLED WITH MORE OF YOU!

October 31: God Save Me

Cultivating the character and nature of God can be challenging. There are so many things we grapple with in our lives – our past, family challenges, and the uncertainty of the future that distracts and puts us in a state of confusion.

"I don't really understand myself, for I want to do what is right, but I don't do it. Instead, I do what I hate." (Romans 7:15)

Pray:

- My God and Father, save me from every distraction and self-destruction!
- My God empowers me to grow in your nature, in every area of my life through the power of the Holy Spirit, in Jesus' name!

MEDITATION FOR THE DAY:

 HOLY SPIRIT, THANK YOU FOR SAVING ME, IN THE NAME OF JESUS!

November 1: Six, Seven Things

Happy new month dear friends and family! God, your Father, the one who made us, and destined us to have rulership of the earth is mighty and worthy of your praise! The best is ahead of you! The secret to accessing the best in God is to be mindful of the things He hates and make a conscious effort to walk in His path.

1. "There are six or seven kinds of people the LORD doesn't like…" (Proverbs 6:16 CEV)

Does God hate people? Not at all! God loves people so much that He gave Jesus for our redemption. However, there are seven things we do that God detests. Join me in the next few days to uncover these things.

Your life is beautiful, LIVE IT!

MEDITATION FOR THE DAY:

HOLY SPIRIT, HELP ME TO LIVE MY LIFE FOR YOUR GLORY!

November 2: Too Proud

At the top of God's list of the things He hates is 'Pride' or 'Proud look'. Being proud is "the attitude that makes one overestimate oneself and discount others." (Proverbs 6:17a AMP). It is not wrong to estimate yourself high, but do not discount others.

1. A lot of people have gone into pride mode unconsciously after their expectations were dashed or wrongly misjudged the actions of others

The danger of pride is the harm it causes. Pride blindfolds you to reasoning and sound judgement. The world will throw unpleasant situations at you, "but the grace that God gives is even stronger. As the scripture says, "God resists the proud, but gives grace to the humble." (James 4:6 GNT).

Submit your pride to God, now!

MEDITATION FOR THE DAY:

HOLY SPIRIT, I SUBMIT MY PRIDE AND MY HEART TO YOU IN JESUS' NAME!

November 3: White Lies

God hates lying! Can you believe that? Yet, the way we tell lies is scary. Some of the biggest ones are what we have termed 'white lies' (telling lies because we do not want someone to get hurt) or 'phone/Social media lies' (representing untrue facts about us and locations).

1. "The LORD hates every liar…" (Proverbs 12:22 CEV)

Lying breaks trust. You will never be taken seriously even when you are speaking the truth. Lying to make others look bad or to avoid the discomfort that comes from being truthful, is not acceptable to God – even to our fellow beings.

God can help you if you sincerely want to stop this habit you hate so much!

MEDITATION FOR THE DAY:

HOLY SPIRIT, I REPENT FROM MY HABIT OF TELLING LIES. HELP ME TO BE TRUTHFUL ALWAYS, IN JESUS' NAME!

November 4: Killing Others

The thought of seeing others dead or even carrying out the act of killing them – God hates. The wickedness of our hearts would wish to see those who hurt or cause us harm suffer pain too, rather than resolve the conflict points.

1. "You have heard that people were told in the past, 'Do not commit murder; anyone who does will be brought to trial." (Matthew 5:21 GNT)

2. "But I say, if you are even angry with someone, you are subject to judgement! If you call someone an idiot, you are in danger of being brought before the court. And if you curse someone, you are in danger of the fires of hell." (Matthew 5:22 NLT)

Physical murder is bad, but God sees killing others beyond wanting them physically dead.

The state of your heart, and the words you utter can kill.

MEDITATION FOR THE DAY:

HOLY SPIRIT, HELP ME TO FORGIVE OTHERS WHEN THEY HURT ME, IN JESUS' NAME!

November 5: Wicked Heart

Our heart remains the center of pursuit for the operations of good, and evil intents. God desires to be the driving force of your life; the devil seeks to be the Master of It. What goes on in your heart matters to God. Your heart reveals you!

1. "The human heart is the most deceitful of all things, and desperately wicked. Who really knows how bad it is? (Jeremiah 17:9 NLT)

No one except God knows the intentions and motives in your heart. He knows all your plans and wants to bring them to pass. But God hates "a heart that plots wicked schemes" (Proverbs 6:18a HCSB).

Anytime you think of hurting others or intentionally rejoice over their downfall, wickedness is at play. And God gives no peace to the wicked!

MEDITATION FOR THE DAY:

HOLY SPIRIT, RENEW MY HEART TO SEE OTHERS, THE WAY, YOU SEE THEM.

November 6: Evil to Others

The thoughts of cursing injury, harm, and hurt to others, comes naturally to some people. They live and thrive when others are troubled, suffering, and experiencing misfortune. God hates such kind of people who rejoice at the pains of others.

1. "The thoughts of evil people are disgusting to the LORD…" (Proverbs 15:26 GWT)

This act of humanity is on the increase. The thirst for evil and the destruction of others is alarming. To overcome this unavoidable practice of witchcraft, let God be your God! Never take yourself out of the covering of the blood of Jesus. Let the Holy Spirit guide your paths.

The days are evil! Please, read and meditate on Psalms 91.

MEDITATION FOR THE DAY:

HOLY SPIRIT, PROTECT ME AND ALL THAT CONCERNS FROM THE EVIL OF OUR WORLD, IN JESUS' NAME!

November 7: A False Witness

Every matter or human activity that takes place on earth has a witness or witnesses. The view of the witness may be true or false. A false witness breathes out lies (even half-truths), about what he or she heard or saw. God hates such people!

1. "You shall not give false testimony against your neighbor" (Exodus 20:16 NIV)

Anyone who gives a wrong testimony about others, or an account of any human activity creates schism, hatred, and enmity among people. People who do this, tend to seek the favor of others, not knowing they are taking themselves out of God's favor.

Be careful how you report what you saw or heard. God is watching!

MEDITATION FOR THE DAY:

HOLY SPIRIT, HELP ME TO BE A TRUE WITNESS OF EVENTS, IN JESUS' NAME!

November 8: Stop the Slander

There are six things which the LORD hates, yes, seven which are an abomination to Him: one sending forth contentions between brethren." (Proverbs 6:17, 19 KJV and YLT). When you slander others, you are breaking a core part of God's teaching:

1. "Brothers and sisters stop slandering each other. Those who slander and judge other believers' slander and judge God's teachings. If you judge God's teachings, you are no longer following them. Instead, you are judging them." (James 4:11 GWT)

God hates this character flaw. Do not say cruel things about others! God is asking for a turnaround, from these seven things that He hates!

Yes, YOU CAN!

MEDITATION FOR THE DAY:

HOLY SPIRIT, I RECEIVE YOUR GRACE, TO MAKE A TURNAROUND FROM THESE SEVEN CHARACTER FLAWS, IN JESUS' NAME!

November 9: Enmity with God

The hostility, opposition, and disdain the world has towards the idea or existence of God is threatening. This state of our human mind is bringing unbearable pains, hurt, hardships, destruction, and disasters to us.

1. "You adulterers and adulteresses, do you not know that friendship with the world is hostility toward God? Therefore, whoever wants to be a friend of the world makes himself an enemy of God." (James 4:4 NHEB)

Pray:

My God and Father, I will forever give you the first place in my life above the affairs of this world, in Jesus' name!

MEDITATION FOR THE DAY:

HOLY SPIRIT, CHANGE ME TO FULFIL GOD'S PURPOSE ON EARTH IN JESUS' NAME!

November 10: Spiritual Gift

Apostle Paul, in his writing to the church in Corinthians, noted his concern about the possible ignorance they had about spiritual gifts. That same concern is a worry to us today. The understanding and place of spiritual gifts are being misused.

1. Spiritual gifts are the special endowments given by the Holy Spirit for the "common good" (1 Corinthians 12:1a, 7b AMP)

But in our world today, spiritual gifts are being used for personal profitability, to create unnecessary fears in others, and to make a demi-god out of a mortal man or woman.

Let us take a trip together, in the next few days, to rediscover these gifts, their uses, and the ones you have been given!

MEDITATION FOR THE DAY:

HOLY SPIRIT, REVEAL THE MYSTERIES OF YOUR GIFTS TO ME, IN JESUS' NAME!

November 11: Wisdom Gift

Life can be complex with all the race for survival, the troubles, and the distractions that clog our path. The desire to know what to do, how to go about life issues, and making the right decisions can be difficult if we lack the wisdom gift.

1. "Wisdom is the ability to make good judgements based on what you have learned from your experience or the knowledge and understanding that gives you this ability" (Cambridge dictionary)

The display and appeal of human wisdom have shown that we rarely learn from our experiences – many of us end up repeating our past mistakes. Wisdom has its origin: "The beginning of wisdom is to fear the LORD…" (Proverbs 9:10 NET Bible).

Honoring God and His word give you unusual access to wisdom for all issues of life.

MEDITATION FOR THE DAY: HOLY SPIRIT, I RECEIVE THE SPIRIT OF THE FEAR OF THE LORD.

November 12: Knowledge Gift

There is nothing so soothing to the human soul as having great knowledge of things. How sweet it is to be knowledgeable, but how limited we are, about the things we can have knowledge of. What then makes the gift of knowledge differ from just having knowledge?

1. "The Word of Knowledge is the supernatural revelation of the Holy Ghost of certain facts in the mind of God"

There is no amount of experience or knowledge we acquire that can help us resolve some of the most challenging situations in our lives.

But having access to God's gift of knowledge shall always give you stability. (Isaiah 33:6 NKJV)

MEDITATION FOR THE DAY:

HOLY SPIRIT, I RECEIVE YOUR SPIRIT OF KNOWLEDGE IN JESUS' NAME!

November 13: Wonder Working Faith

Anything and almost everything around us threatens or shakes our foundation on the possibility of seeing our hopes and expectations come to pass. We pray yet doubt if the prayers will come to pass.

1. "Now faith is the assurance (title deed, confirmation) of things hoped for (divinely guaranteed), and the evidence of things not seen [the conviction of their reality—faith comprehends as fact what cannot be experienced by the physical senses]." (Hebrews 11:1 AMP)

Oh, yes, you have prayed so long, believed so long, waited so long. The gift of faith helps you to break limits and change your perspective.

We experience faith-wreck when we don't seek and understand God's perspective. Faith is seeking God's view and acting on it!

MEDITATION FOR THE DAY:

HOLY SPIRIT, I RECEIVE THE GIFT OF FAITH TO SURMOUNT LIFE'S CHALLENGES!

November 14: Extraordinary Healing

Do we still believe that divine healing exists? Has the death of a sick loved one and the existence of pain or condition in your life, made you throw the thoughts of supernatural healing out of the window? I struggled with this for some time too!

1. "To others the Spirit has given... the power to heal the sick." (1 Corinthians 12:9)

Dear friends and family, there is still power given to us to heal the sick (the healer – Jesus is alive!). O how I long for the demonstration of these gifts of healing in your life and mine. The intake of pills and the strange names of illnesses coupled with the doctors' prescriptions are scary. "Dear friend, I pray that you may enjoy good health..." (3 John 1:2 NIV).

All kinds of sicknesses – mental, emotional, spiritual, physical, or even financial, keep you and your loved ones incapacitated.

MEDITATION FOR THE DAY:

HOLY SPIRIT, I RECEIVE THE GIFT OF HEALING IN MY LIFE AND FOR OTHERS IN JESUS' NAME!

November 15: Sudden Change

There are so many things going on in our lives, families, and environment which we cannot control or find a way through. But deep within us, we know with the intervention of the supernatural, there can be a sudden change.

1. The gift of doing miracles is given, to enable us to carry out acts that are contrary to natural laws, with power beyond human capacity (Daystar 300L material)

"He gives one person the power to perform miracles..." (1 Corinthians 12:10a NLT). God wants your life to be filled with miracles daily. "...the person who believes in me will perform the miraculous deeds that I am doing and will perform greater deeds than these... (John 14:12 NET Bible). This is true – walk in it!

MEDITATION FOR THE DAY:

HOLY SPIRIT, I RECEIVE THE GIFT OF MIRACULOUS DEEDS FOR DAILY LIVING IN JESUS' NAME!

November 16: Seeing Beyond the Present

Within everyone resides a longing to know what the present and the future hold. This human tendency has made us develop itchy ears and craving hearts, to pursue those we believe can tell the future or what is happening in our lives. Prophecy is a gift from the Holy Spirit to:

1. Foretell the future.
2. Speak a new message from God to the people. (1 Corinthians 12:10 AMP)

God gives prophecies "for edification [to promote spiritual growth], speak words of encouragement [to uphold and advise others concerning the matters of God] and speak words of consolation [to compassionately comfort others] - (1 Corinthians 14:3).

Friends desire this gift – your life will be filled with God's love and power!

MEDITATION FOR THE DAY:

HOLY SPIRIT, I RECEIVE THE GIFT OF PROPHECY FOR LIFE MASTERY, IN JESUS' NAME!

November 17: Sensitivity to Spirits

There are over 7 billion people on earth with different aspirations, dreams, plans, and thoughts. Some have good intentions, while many have negative intentions. How do you know when others have good intentions toward you?

1. Their actions and not their words toward you (action they say, speaks louder than words).
2. Through the manifestation of the discernment of spirits given to you by the Holy Spirit.

Sensitivity of spirits is "...the ability to discern and distinguish between [the utterances of true] spirits [and false ones]". (1 Corinthians 12:10c AMPC).

We are spirit-being capable of true and false utterances. But through the gift of discernment, you can rest assured on how to respond and God's protection!

MEDITATION FOR THE DAY:

HOLY SPIRIT, I RECEIVE THE GIFT OF DISTINGUISHING BETWEEN SPIRITS, IN JESUS' NAME!

November 18: Tongues and Interpretation

The how and why of these gifts remain a subject of contention even among Christians. Unbelievers wonder – this is gibberish, madness, or drunkenness! When you speak in tongue you edify yourself, when you can interpret, you edify others.

1. "Those who speak in strange tongues do not speak to others but to God, because no one understands them. They are speaking secret truths by the power of the Spirit". (1 Corinthians 14:2 GNT).

It is good to speak in tongues as the Holy Spirit gives us utterance, it will be more beneficial if we can interpret. Speaking in tongues is a great weapon of spiritual warfare and the building-up of your faith in difficult times.

Ask for these gifts today!

MEDITATION FOR THE DAY:

HOLY SPIRIT, I RECEIVE THE GIFTS OF SPEAKING AND INTERPRETATION OF TONGUES, IN JESUS' NAME!

November 19: Discover your Gifts

God has given each one of us unique spiritual gifts to be a blessing to others and our world. Spiritual gifts give you a great advantage in life. They make you valuable, useful to others, and productive in your area of strength and purpose.

1. "Let love be your highest goal! But you should also desire the special abilities the Spirit gives…" (1 Corinthians 14:1 NLT)

MEDITATION FOR THE DAY:

HOLY SPIRIT REVEAL YOUR UNIQUE GIFTS IN MY LIFE FOR THE BENEFIT OF OTHERS, AND MY RELEVANCE IN LIFE, IN JESUS' NAME!

November 20: Transforming Words

The 26 alphabets taught in schools have a dynamic influence on our world today. No matter the language or tongue we speak, they are made up of at least one consonant or a mix of consonants or vowels that can make or mar your day. Words become our reality, just as the word God says

"For the word of God is living and active and full of power [making it operative, energizing, and effective]. It is sharper than any two-edged sword, penetrating as far as the division of the soul and spirit [the completeness of a person] and of both joints and marrow [the deepest parts of our nature], exposing and judging the very thoughts and intentions of the heart." (Hebrew 4:12 Amplified)

Amazing, what words can do! Let's take a trip for the next nine days, examining the characters of the transforming word of God in our lives and the world!

MEDITATION FOR THE DAY:

HOLY SPIRIT, REVEAL THE MYSTERIES IN THE WORD OF GOD TO ME, IN JESUS' NAME!

November 21: Living Word

Every word we speak has life in them. No word ever spoken is idle of its effect and impact. Our word has breath – and the capacity to give life or snuff life out of others or any situation. Even God's living word is in your neighborhood:

1. "The Word became flesh and blood and moved into the neighborhood..." (John 1:14a MSG)

Every word God spoke and wrote through men inspired by the Holy Spirit has life in them. They will always come to pass! Why? The word of God has the seal of His son Jesus – His blood is the highest guarantee that every word of God concerning you will come to pass!

Dive deep into the living-word today!

MEDITATION FOR THE DAY:

HOLY SPIRIT, LET YOUR LIVING WORD PREVAIL IN MY LIFE, IN JESUS' NAME!

November 22: Power in Words

Each time we speak, the words or contents we utter causes some form of changes, reactions, or responses. This is happening because the words we speak have power behind them – whether positive or negative. The words you speak change things.

1. "For the word of God is… full of power [making it operative, energizing, and effective]." (Hebrews 4:12a AMP)

The power behind our words makes them operational, energizing, and effective at any level that we use them. The word of God in your mouth carries life and power.

Those same words created the universe, they will also create and form your world!

MEDITATION FOR THE DAY:

HOLY SPIRIT, LET YOUR WORD DWELL RICHLY IN ME, IN JESUS' NAME!

November 23: Sharpness in Words

Communication is incomplete when parties involved do not understand the thoughts and concepts being exchanged. People always respond based on the sharpness (intensity, harshness, or clarity) of words you communicate to them.

1. "The word of God... is sharper than any two-edged sword, penetrating as far as the division of the soul and spirit [the completeness of a person], and of both joints and marrow [the deepest parts of our nature], exposing and judging the very thoughts and intentions of the heart." (Hebrew 4:12 AMP)

When you relate with others, they see the clarity, intensity, or harshness of your words. The intensity and alertness of God's words are what make them penetrate our body, soul, and spirit.

Your words also have the same ability – be mindful of them!

MEDITATION FOR THE DAY: HOLY SPIRIT, LET THE SHARPNESS OF MY WORDS BRING HEALING TO OTHERS IN JESUS' NAME!

November 24: Word Invasion

We are living in a time where the impact of technology is invading our life with information, thoughts, concepts, and ideas that are controlling us. The overload of information or words that you expose yourself to is controlling your actions.

1. "Let Christ's word with all its wisdom and richness live in you..." (Colossians 3:16)

Whose words are invading your life? The words of men or the words of God? The impact of the words you hear or listen to tells how you react or respond to the issues in your life.

Let the written and spoken words of Christ invade your life today!

MEDITATION FOR THE DAY:

HOLY SPIRIT, LET THE MESSAGE ABOUT CHRIST COMPLETELY FILL MY LIFE, IN JESUS' NAME!

November 25: Bitter-Sweet Words

The power and beauty of our regenerated mind is the ability to control our words. But the case is the reverse today. We have lost the discipline of word-control. Our words are invested in tearing down others more than building them up.

1. "Words of thanksgiving and cursing pour out from the same mouth. My friends, this should not happen!" (James 3:10 GNT)

I know it is hard to restrain ourselves from not using derogatory and harsh words on others, especially when they hurt or disappoint us.

Our maturity is displayed when we hold back the bitter words welling up in our hearts. At such moments, yield to the Holy Spirit to help you, and subject you under His control.

MEDITATION FOR THE DAY:

HOLY SPIRIT, I RECEIVE YOUR HELP TO CONTROL MY WORDS, IN JESUS' NAME!

November 26: Words Judge You

The test of our character is in our ability to use our words constructively. In our world today, many of us are increasingly becoming unconscious of the negative impact about what we say, can do to us.

1. "Your words will be used to judge you--to declare you either innocent or guilty." (Matthew 12:37 GNT)

It is true and you must believe it, that people will have a better sense of who you are through the words you speak before they can decide if you are the type of individual to invest time and resources in. You can consciously watch what you say through your inner processing of what the effect or impact of what you say will have in each situation. Many people are in a bad position today because they were careless with their words.

Your words judge you daily, watch what you say!

MEDITATION FOR THE DAY:

HOLY SPIRIT, HELP ME TO BE MINDFUL OF MY WORDS, IN JESUS' NAME!

November 27: Flawless

A known fact about us as spirit beings is our weaknesses and imperfections manifested through the deceitfulness of our motives. Everything we say or do is always robbed of by greed, selfishness, and wickedness of heart.

1. "Every word of God is flawless...". (Proverbs 30:5 Berean Study Bible)

We do not mean what we say to ourselves 85% of the time. Our words are flawed because our motives are not always right. With God – you can go to sleep with whatever He has said to you or what is written in the Bible.

"All you say can be trusted; your teachings are true and will last forever." (Psalms 119:160 CEV).

MEDITATION FOR THE DAY:

HOLY SPIRIT, HELP ME BUILD MY LIFE ON YOUR FLAWLESS WORDS, IN JESUS' NAME!

November 28: Life-Giving Spirit

The nature of a person is largely experienced by what comes out of him or her. That nature is formed from a relationship with a superior personality whose traits are manifested.

1. So, it is written [in Scripture], "The first MAN, Adam, BECAME A LIVING SOUL (an individual);" the last Adam (Christ) became a life-giving spirit [restoring the dead to life]. – 1 Corinthians 15:45 (Amplified)

When Christ lives in you, you are no longer an ordinary person living to exist, you become a person whose life brings blessing and hope to others.

The evidence of Christ living in you – is the word of God through the presence of the Holy Spirit.

MEDITATION FOR THE DAY:

I AM A LIFE-GIVING SPIRIT THROUGH THE PRESENCE OF THE WORD OF GOD AND THE HOLY SPIRIT LIVING IN ME!

November 29: Change Your World

In the last 300 days of putting these daily devotionals together, one thing remained so strong in my heart – "words can shape your world".

1. "By faith, we understand that the universe was created by the word of God, so that what is seen was not made out of things that are visible". (Hebrews 11:3 ESV)

Your life is open for change if only you use the right words – especially what God says about you. "The word is very near thee, in thy mouth, and in thine heart, and in thine hands to do it". (Deuteronomy 30:14 BST). No excuses!

Pray:

I will shape my life and my world daily by what God says about me. (Read the bible daily, pray with them, and ask the Holy Spirit to help you).

MEDITATION FOR THE DAY:

I AM WHAT GOD SAYS I AM; I HAVE WHAT HE SAYS I HAVE IN JESUS' NAME!

November 30: Word-Formation

You can profoundly change things in your life and environment! The composition of every statement and phrase you make can be deliberately and consciously formed to see the results you desire in your life

1. "The word that saves is right here, as near as the tongue in your mouth, as close as the heart in your chest. It's the word of faith that welcomes God to go to work and set things right for us". (Romans 10:8 Message)

The use of God's word is a free platform to form the right words we need to get results in our lives. Please, let the words of God be the foundation for your WORD-FORMATION!
Pray:

The word of God is the foundation of my words – no more using fear-filled words!

MEDITATION FOR THE DAY:

I AM AN EXPRESSION OF THE WORD OF GOD!

December 1: Increasing Faith

The quality of life we live is a by-product of our beliefs, actions, and inactions. Wherever you are now, what you believed, the actions you took, and the ones you did not take got you there. Do you believe in God? You do not? The substance is formed!

1. "...Faith comprehends as fact what cannot be experienced with the physical senses..." (Hebrew 11:1b AMP)

Every being created by God has been given the ability to birth into reality the visions, desires, and thoughts they want to see manifest in their lives. For those who believe in God – your faith is an inherent trust and confidence in the power, wisdom, and goodness of God.

We will be looking at some faith dimensions in the next few days. Having faith in God makes all the difference in life...

MEDITATION FOR THE DAY:

HOLY SPIRIT, INCREASE MY FAITH IN GOD, IN JESUS' NAME!

December 2: Victorious Through Faith

One common denominator for everyone one of us, no matter our social strata, culture, or nationality, is the many battles we contend with in life. The contentions and restraints we experience, especially from evil forces, are unimaginable.

1. "For every child of God defeats this evil world, and we achieve this victory through our faith". (1 John 5:4 NLT)

Humanity is the ultimate of God's creation. The ones that acknowledge the domain of God in their lives are targets of the enemy. However, we have been guaranteed victory not just in that situation, but over the whole world.

Your faith in God brings the world to your feet! Strive to increase your faith level, today...

MEDITATION FOR THE DAY:

HOLY SPIRIT, I AM A CHILD OF GOD, I'M VICTORIOUS ALWAYS, IN JESUS' NAME!

December 3: Faith Fuels Fate

I stumbled upon an article about facts on global poverty. More than 3 billion people — live on less than $2.50 a day. More than 1.3 billion live in extreme poverty — less than $1.25 a day. That is more than 70% of people in the world living in poverty. These statistics apply to many other areas of our lives

1. Fate may have brought many to poverty or despair, but faith can take many from poverty and despair to a life of abundance

The challenges in life and the uncertainties that plague us can drain the possibilities of a great destiny. Hard work is good, but smart work is being diligent and trusting in Him that makes a bleak future bright.

"God lifts the poor and needy from dust and ashes" (Psalms 113:7 CEV). Your faith determines your fate!

MEDITATION FOR THE DAY:

HOLY SPIRIT, MY FUTURE IS BRIGHT IN YOU, IN JESUS' NAME!

December 4: Obedience Activates Faith

The possibilities in life are unimaginable! But how to reach them seems a tall order for many of us. The strength or faith to achieve the things that we desire is weakened by fear of the unknown, our past experiences, and the state of our heart

1. Life's greatest therapy comes from the words we hear and allow into our lives

Faith comes from obeying words – especially in the words of an omnipotent God. Every word of God carries life that transforms any situation.

When you do what it says, your faith increases to see the manifestation of your desires. "…Listen! Obedience is better than sacrifice…" (1 Samuel 15:22 NLT)

MEDITATION FOR THE DAY:

HOLY SPIRIT, I YIELD MYSELF TO OBEYING YOUR WORDS, IN JESUS' NAME!

December 5: Faith Fuels Giving

There are principles and laws that govern the universe. One of these laws is the law of giving. Giving is one act many of us struggle with. It does not matter how much or how plentiful we have; it is always a struggle to give to others or give to a course.

1. "God will make you rich enough so that you can always be generous." (2 Corinthians 9:11a GWT)

The expression of our faith in God for what we have is found in our acts of giving. "What do you have that God hasn't given you? And if everything you have is from God, why boast as though it were not a gift?" (1 Corinthians 4:7b & c NLT).

When it comes to giving, you can never get it wrong. Your giving creates an open heaven!

MEDITATION FOR THE DAY:

HOLY SPIRIT, HELP ME TO INCREASE IN MY GENEROSITY, IN JESUS' NAME!

December 6: Evil Hates Faith

The twins - fear and doubt, are two emotional touch points that give access to the prevalence of evil operations in our lives. Evil thrives when faith in God is diminished for faith in man, our human abilities, and successes.

1. "Let your faith be like a shield, and you will be able to stop all the flaming arrows of the evil one." (Ephesians 6:16 CEV)

It is glaring that enemies will never stop flaming their arrows of evil against you. And it is hard to defeat them with our human strength. Evil perpetrators hate those who have faith in God.

If you do not have faith and confidence in God, you will become prey to the antics and destruction of the devil.

Take up your shield of faith now!

MEDITATION FOR THE DAY:

HOLY SPIRIT, FORTIFY MY SHIELD OF FAITH, IN JESUS' NAME!

December 7: Faith Connects Divinity

The state of distress, confusion, and uncertainties we go through has driven many to places where we have lost hope, and confidence for the future. Our quest for human solutions has taken us far from the easy help we can get from divinity.

1. "And it is impossible to please God without faith. Anyone who wants to come to him must believe that God exists and that he rewards those who sincerely seek him." (Ephesians 6:16 CEV)

The help of mankind is in divinity – God the Father, Jesus Christ, and the Holy Spirit. In one sync, they created the world. They know the pathway to resolve all the issues that confront you.

Seek Him diligently and sincerely today!

MEDITATION FOR THE DAY:

HOLY SPIRIT, CONNECT MY FAITH TO THE POWER OF DIVINITY, IN JESUS' NAME!

December 8: Your Faith Commands

Dear family and friends, the outcomes that can take place in your life are truly in God's control but hinged on your faith in Him (confidence and trust). God has designed the world to be at the command of your faith and the things you say.

1. "I can guarantee this truth: This is what will be done for someone who doesn't doubt but believes what he says will happen: He can say to this mountain, 'Be uprooted and thrown into the sea,' and it will be done for him." (Mark 11:23 GWT)

You cannot rise above the words you say.

Your faith causes the world to be at your feet. Your faith increases by hearing and doing what God says! Say what God says!

MEDITATION FOR THE DAY:

HOLY SPIRIT, I RECEIVE WHAT GOD SAYS WITH A NOBLE HEART, IN JESUS' NAME!

December 9: Faith Breaks Impossibilities

Jesus Christ's statement to Jairus (a leader whose daughter was confirmed dead in Israel), still holds for you and me today: "Jesus said to him, "As far as possibilities go, everything is possible for the person who believes." (Mark 9:23 GWT).

1. "Do not be afraid any longer; only believe and trust [in Me and have faith in My ability to do this], and she will be made well." (Luke 8:50b Amplified). God can turn your situation around. Only believe He can!

Pray:

Holy Spirit, increase my faith in your ability to do great things in my life

MEDITATION FOR THE DAY:

NOTHING SHALL BE IMPOSSIBLE FOR ME TO ACCOMPLISH THROUGH THE HOLY SPIRIT WHO EMPOWERS ME IN JESUS' NAME!

December 10: End of Days

I was having a phone conversation with a friend, and we got into talking about the troubles, chaos, and uncertainties in the world, especially with the state of the church globally. I told him I was not surprised because Jesus Christ did not leave us clueless about what is happening in the world and the church.

1. "Many will come and claim to be me. They will say they are the Messiah, and they will fool many people... You will soon hear about wars and threats of wars, but do not be afraid... Evil will spread and cause many people to stop loving others". (Matthew 24:5-6, 12 CEV). Please read the whole chapter.

This series is to bring to our consciousness the reality of the end of days, and what is expected of us to make sure we are not caught unguarded.

The end time is not a hoax.

MEDITATION FOR THE DAY:

HOLY SPIRIT, KEEP MY EYES AND HEART ON YOU IN THESE LAST DAYS, IN JESUS' NAME!

December 11: Global Conflicts

Jesus said that in the last days "you will continually hear about wars and rumors of wars... for nation will rise against nation, and kingdom against kingdom..." (Matthew 24:6-7 Amplified). Certainly, this is obvious to us. What should we do?

1. "See that you are not frightened, for those things must take place... (Matthew 24:6b NASB)

It is amazing yet unsettling how Christ wants us to respond to global conflicts. There must be a way to thrive amidst human conflicts:

"I've told you this so that my peace will be with you. In the world you will have trouble. But cheer up! I have overcome the world." (John 16:33 GWT).

Christ in you, is the solution!

MEDITATION FOR THE DAY:

HOLY SPIRIT, KEEP MY EYES AND HEART ON YOU AMIDST GLOBAL CONFLICTS, IN JESUS' NAME!

December 12: Increased Lawlessness

Jesus said that in the last days, "because lawlessness is increased, the love of most people will grow cold" (Matthew 24:12 Amplified). The nations of the earth are experiencing an unimaginable state of disorder in one area or the other. We break rules expecting no consequences for our actions or inaction.

1. "If you dig a pit, you fall in it; if you break through a wall, a snake bites you" (Ecclesiastes 10:8 GNT)

Life is governed by laws, principles, ordinances, commands, and precepts. We can never break the laws (whether the ones put in place by man or by God), instead, the law breaks us when we disregard them!

The signs of the end of days are here and it's real!

MEDITATION FOR THE DAY:

HOLY SPIRIT, I YIELD MY HEART TO KEEP YOUR LAWS, IN JESUS NAME!

December 13: Dangerous Times

The end of days comes with great dangerous times. These times will be experienced with great stress, troubles, and difficult situations that will be hard to bear. We are already seeing the outward expressions of these times. Some of them are:

1. "People will be selfish and love money. They will brag, be arrogant, and use abusive language. They will curse their parents, show no gratitude, have no respect for what is holy…" (2 Timothy 3:2 GWT)

Can you attest to the above? The dark side of us will be at play. And there is nothing you can do if your life is not in divine alignment with God.

We are prone to the dangers of the end of the last days. Let your life be controlled by God alone.

MEDITATION FOR THE DAY:

HOLY SPIRIT, MY LIFE IS YOURS; SAVE ME FROM THESE DANGEROUS TIMES, IN JESUS' NAME!

December 14: Toxic Humanity

We were created in the image of God and designed to exhibit the character of God in our communication, and relationship with others. We are so far from this today. Our humanity is mixed with toxic nature that manifests signs of the end of days:

1. [and they will be] unloving [devoid of natural human affection, calloused and inhumane], irreconcilable, malicious gossips, devoid of self-control [intemperate, immoral], brutal, haters of good

The scariest of this is when leaders promote hatred, fear, and unforgiveness among the citizens or congregation. We have replaced cultivating godly nature with "an eye for an eye".

Beware not to be caught up with the devil's antics in these last days.

MEDITATION FOR THE DAY:

HOLY SPIRIT, EXAMINE MY LIFE, REMOVE EVERY TOXIC NATURE, IN JESUS' NAME!

December 15: Deception

The end of days is with us, its signs and pangs are felt on a global scale. Global conflicts, famines, earthquakes, sudden destruction of natural habitats (Amazon and California), and illnesses are glaring to us. Another sign is "DECEPTION"

1. "Jesus answered them, "Be careful not to let anyone deceive you." (Matthew 24:4 GWT)

Deception is the act of causing someone to accept as true or valid what is false or invalid (Merriam-Webster). Many young people and adults are being deceived to engage in acts that will be destructive to them. Peer pressure can mostly be an act of deception.

Dear friend, beware of what you accept as truth. If it lacks the virtues of God, you are about to be deceived.

MEDITATION FOR THE DAY:

HOLY SPIRIT, HELP ME TO BE DISCERNING OF FALSEHOOD, IN JESUS' NAME!

December 16: Lovers of Pleasure

God is all-knowing and strategic in how He has fashioned our nature. One adorable nature He gave to us is the ability to enjoy pleasure – a feeling of happiness, satisfaction, and enjoyment. We were even created for His pleasure (Rev 4:11c AKJV). But in these last days, we are now:

1. "lovers of pleasure rather than lovers of God". (2 Timothy 3:4b NIV)

Our feeling of happiness, satisfaction, and enjoyment no longer comes from God. Our pleasures come from the pursuits of power, money, sex, entertainment, social media, and success.

God wants you to be happy and to enjoy your life, but not at the expense of destroying others and your life in eternity.

Christ is coming soon!

MEDITATION FOR THE DAY:

HOLY SPIRIT, INCREASE MY LOVE FOR DIVINITY, IN JESUS' NAME!

December 17: Jesus is Coming

The return of Jesus to earth is one subject that 86% of the world's population struggles to accept or believe. Many generations have come and gone, and yet Christ is yet to come – the sinfulness and wickedness of man are on the increase.

1. "So then, you also must always be ready, because the Son of Man will come at an hour when you are not expecting him." (Matthew 24:44 GNT)

Everything is built by someone, but the builder of all things is God. Life is designed for feedback. For everything you and I do on earth, we will surely give an account of them.

The happenings at the end of days are ushering in the return of Jesus Christ. He will come like a thief in the night. Repent and yield to God today!

MEDITATION FOR THE DAY:

HOLY SPIRIT, LET MY LIFE BE WORTHY OF YOUR KINGDOM, IN JESUS' NAME!

December 18: Do not be Distracted

The busyness, activities, and pursuit of what to eat, drink, wear and own are distracting many of us about the reality of the second coming of Jesus Christ. Do not let us be distracted, hear what Jesus said (Luke 17:26-30 NLT)

1. "When the Son of Man returns, it will be like it was in Noah's day. In those days, the people enjoyed banquets and parties and weddings right up to the time Noah entered his boat and the flood came and destroyed them all.

"And the world will be as it was in the days of Lot. People went about their daily business—eating and drinking, buying, and selling, farming, and building... Yes, it will be 'business as usual' right up to the day when the Son of Man is revealed.

Jesus Christ is coming soon. Are you prepared to meet with Him?

MEDITATION FOR THE DAY:

HOLY SPIRIT, HELP ME TO LIVE MY LIFE DAILY, IN PREPARATION FOR JESUS' SECOND COMING!

December 19: Your Safety

The pains, anguish, sorrows, disappointments, and struggles being experienced at the end of days, and those at the coming of Christ cannot be escaped. Your safety and mine are in the name of the Lord.

"Then whoever calls on the name of the LORD will be saved". (Joel 2:32 GWT)

Pray:

Holy Spirit, let the mercies of Jesus preserve and protect me in these last days

Holy Spirit, I present and yield my body to you in these last days

MEDITATION FOR THE DAY:

HOLY SPIRIT, FILL ME WITH YOUR LOVE AND PRESENCE, SEEK AND SAVE THE LOST THROUGH ME IN THESE LAST DAYS, IN JESUS' NAME!

December 20: Planning

Achieving the purposes of God for us requires planning guided by the Holy Spirit. Planning is the process of thinking about the activities required to achieve the desired goal. It is the first and foremost activity to achieve desired results. (Wikipedia)

1. Every dream, vision, or aspiration is intangible or invincible. Planning helps to bring your dream, vision, or aspiration to fruition

2. Effective planning helps you to count the cost and equips you with the information needed to actualize what God has shown or told you.

"If one of you is planning to build a tower, you sit down first and figure out what it will cost, to see if you have enough money to finish the job". (Luke 14:28).

What are your desired results for the new year? Planning is one effective tool that will help you achieve them.

MEDITATION FOR THE DAY:

HOLY SPIRIT, REVEAL YOUR PLANS FOR MY LIFE & IN THE NEW YEAR, IN JESUS' NAME!

December 21: Dreams + Visions + Planning

Planning as a process cannot be successful without the fueling of a dream or vision. Planning is an exercise in futility if your heart is empty of what can be done better, whose life needs to be changed, and what the future could be.

1. "Without a Vision is a people made naked..."
   (Proverbs 29:18 YLT)

Dreams and visions are the raw materials you need to execute an effective plan. Dreams and visions are given to us by God, captured through our past experiences, taken upon due to the sufferings of others, and driven by the need to see people, processes, and systems work efficiently.

What is your dream? What is your vision?

MEDITATION FOR THE DAY:

HOLY SPIRIT, OPEN MY HEART TO RECEIVE YOUR DREAMS AND VISIONS FOR MY LIFE IN JESUS' NAME!

December 22: Goal Setting + Planning (1)

Planning generates multiple things you can do when your dreams or visions are clarified. However, your plans can become ineffective if you do not have S.M.A.R.T goals to achieve them. "I will give you my message in the form of a vision. Write it clearly enough to be read at a glance..." (Habakkuk 2:2b CEV). Let us look at two of them today:

1. Specific - Your goals should be direct, detailed, and meaningful
2. Measurable – Your goals should be quantifiable to track progress or success

Good planning and hard work lead to prosperity (Proverbs 21:5a NLT). Set goals!

MEDITATION FOR THE DAY:

HOLY SPIRIT, I RECEIVE SMART GOALS TO ACHIEVE YOUR PLANS FOR MY LIFE, IN JESUS' NAME!

December 23: Goal setting + Planning (2)

Many of us struggle with the concept of goal setting. We do not believe in it; we leave it to chance or assign the responsibilities to God. God truly decides the outcomes, but He does not do the planning for you. Let us look at the last part of 'SMART':

3.   Achievable – You should have access to tools and resources to achieve them.

4.   Relevant – Your goals should align with your dreams, visions, and aspirations.

5.   Time-Based – Your goals should have a deadline. "A person plans his course, but the LORD directs his steps". (Proverbs 16:9 NET Bible). Please make plans and set goals that will help you achieve your dreams and visions. (*We can work with you to develop your vision and goals. Please send me a mail*)

MEDITATION FOR THE DAY:

HOLY SPIRIT, I RECEIVE SMART GOALS TO ACHIEVE YOUR PLANS FOR MY LIFE, IN JESUS' NAME!

December 24: Discipline + Planning

Discipline is one word many of us do not want to relate to. We associate limitations, dos, and don'ts with it. Discipline brings control and order to our lives. For your plans to come alive, you need a great measure of control and order in your life.

1. Every athlete in training submits to strict discipline, in order to be crowned with a wreath that will not last; but we do it for one that will last forever. (1 Corinthians 9:25 GNT)

Your life is a serious affair to you, humanity, and God. Your God-given plans have a generational impact. You cannot afford to throw caution to the wind.

You need the discipline to plan, stay with the plan, and see the fulfillment of the plan.

MEDITATION FOR THE DAY:

HOLY SPIRIT, I RECEIVE YOUR GRACE TO STAY WITH YOUR PLANS FOR MY LIFE, IN JESUS' NAME!

December 25: Timing + Planning

In the history of mankind, the events that have impacted our lives positively are the ones that came at the right time. Christmas reminds us of God's plan to save us from the power of sin, sickness, and death!

1. Understanding the timing of the fulfillment of your plans relieves you of the pressures and anxieties of waiting or the experiences of delays.

"The tribe of Issachar supplied 200 leaders, along with all of their relatives under their command. They kept up to date in their understanding of the times and knew what Israel should do." (1 Chronicles 12:32 ISV).

As we make plans, we must understand the time and seasons for their fulfillment. Your alignment with the word of God, consistent communion with the Holy Spirit, and up-to-date knowledge of your environment and assignment, makes a good plan great!

MERRY CHRISTMAS!

MEDITATION FOR THE DAY:

FATHER, LET MY LIFE BE A GIFT TO MY WORLD.

December 26: Patience + Planning

The lack of patience has caused great plans to shipwreck. 99.9% of us struggle with the virtue of PATIENCE. We live in a generation where we expect things to happen in a split second. We need to know that most plans we make take time to materialize.

1. "You need to be patient, in order to do the will of God and receive what he promises". (Hebrews 10:36 GNT)

Many plans go through processes, they operate within principles and laws, and need some level of maturing from you to handle the demand of its outcome.

When you make plans, "stand firm, and you will win life". (Luke 21:19 NIV).

MEDITATION FOR THE DAY:

HOLY SPIRIT, I RECEIVE YOUR SPIRIT OF PERSEVERANCE TO STAY WITH YOUR PLANS FOR MY LIFE, IN JESUS' NAME!

December 27: Prayer + Planning

Prayer is a universal spiritual discipline practiced by many religions in the world. For a Christian, it goes beyond just a ritual, it is a medium of communication and relationship with our heavenly Father. Through prayers, planning is given wings for a flight!

1. "Ask me and I will tell you remarkable secrets you do not know about things to come.". (Jeremiah 33:3 NLT)

When we pray, God's visions and dreams are birthed in our hearts. And through prayers, plans are made and established.

There are forces that contend with the fulfillment of your plans, but with consistent and fervent prayers, the outcome of your plan is guaranteed!

MEDITATION FOR THE DAY:

HOLY SPIRIT, I RECEIVE YOUR SPIRIT OF EFFICACY IN PRAYERS TO ACTUALIZE YOUR PLANS FOR MY LIFE, IN JESUS' NAME!

December 28: Vision and Dream Struggles

Everyone has been given the ability to plan, set goals, and be empowered to achieve their dreams and visions. This is possible because we have an inherent God-nature. But many of us struggle to discover the visions and dreams for our lives.

1. "Before I formed you in the womb, I knew you. Before you were born, I set you apart for my holy purpose..." (Jeremiah 1:5b GWT)

You have a purpose in life. Locked up in your purpose, are the visions and dreams begging to be released through your planning and goal setting. Your life has its visions and dreams.

You were not born to be confused, clueless, or exist to fill a vacuum. I pray that God will open your heart and eyes to see His vision for you!

MEDITATION FOR THE DAY:

HOLY SPIRIT REVEAL TO ME, YOUR VISIONS AND DREAMS FOR MY LIFE, IN JESUS' NAME!

December 29: God Has a Plan

Planning is a God-nature habit. The creation of mankind and all the natural beauty we see on the land, in the sea, and in the air, are God's plan to fulfill His dreams and visions for our planet – earth.

The greatest of these is His plans for you: "I alone know the plans I have for you, plans to bring you prosperity and not disaster, plans to bring about the future you hope for." (Jeremiah 29:11 GNT)

Pray:

Thank you, God, and my Father, for your plans for my life. I choose your plans above all others.

MEDITATION FOR THE DAY:

HOLY SPIRIT, ALIGN MY THOUGHTS, DESIRES, AND ASPIRATIONS TO THE PLANS OF GOD FOR MY LIFE, IN JESUS' NAME!

December 30: The Good Land

Our planet earth has several billion people living in it, with so many vast resources, abundance, and potentials that are enough to go around everyone. But only the richest 1% now owns half of the world's wealth. There must be something they are doing, and there is one thing you too can do. Earth is a good land:

1. If you will obey me, you will eat the good things the land produces (Isaiah 1:19 GNT).

God owns everything in heaven and on earth. He gives access to wealth and riches to whoever He chooses, and to those who obey His principles of abundance.

The land is good, your willingness and obedience to God's laws and principles that govern the earth, are your secrets to any successful year!

MEDITATION FOR THE DAY:

HOLY SPIRIT, I RECEIVE YOUR ACCESS TO THE PRINCIPLES THAT GOVERN THE EARTH IN JESUS' NAME!

December 31: Right Motivation

Living in the time and space of each year and season of life brings opportunities, challenges, and uncertainties. We engage in varying physical and spiritual activities to go through what life brings to our path. In all, our motives drive our results:

1. "Make no mistake about this: You can never make a fool out of God. Whatever you plant is what you'll harvest". (Galatians 6:7 GWT)

Our motives propel the things we do - the things we do are seeds planted, and the harvest we get is determined by the quality of our seeds (motives).

What were your motivations in the outgoing year? What will be your motivations in the in-coming year? Let the laws and principles of God guide your motives all year round!

HAPPY NEW YEAR!

MEDITATION FOR THE DAY:

HOLY SPIRIT, THANK YOU FOR CROWNING MY YEAR WITH YOUR GOODNESS, IN JESUS' NAME!